“As a pastor, I am grate
church. As we all learn how to serve better those who have been hurt in the church but do not leave the church, books like this will prove an invaluable resource.”

—**Jeremy Jenkins**, executive director of All Things All People

“Rather than grow calloused from serving as collateral in the white evangelical machine, Pricelis chose softness and safety. Throughout these pages, she invites readers to see themselves as welcoming sanctuaries to all image bearers, embodying the gospel for every tribe and tongue.”

—**Tiffany Bluhm**, author of *The Women We've Been Waiting For* and *Prey Tell*

“*Being a Sanctuary* is a challenge: a challenge to comfortable Christianity and self-centered faith. Pricelis is not afraid to face complicated, painful topics, including her own story of church hurt and loss, to help Christians become a safe place in a wild world. Being a sanctuary means really seeing people: not just stances and sides but people loved by God who need a truth that sets them free.”

—**Phylicia Masonheimer**, founder and CEO, Every Woman a Theologian

“Within the pages of *Being a Sanctuary*, Pricelis Perreaux-Dominguez lays bare a thought-provoking journey into the essence of Christ's vision for his church. This book sparks a vital discourse on restoration and the true embodiment of what Jesus intended for his community, the Body of Christ. This book is essential reading for those yearning to rediscover a church that embodies the profound love and grace of Christ, offering solace and strength as Psalm 46:1 assures: ‘God is our refuge and strength, an ever-present help in trouble.' This is the strength the church must cling to during its present crisis of apathy."

—**Latasha Morrison**, *New York Times* bestselling author of *Be the Bridge*; CEO and founder of Be the Bridge

"Pricelis's love for the church is matched by her passion for truth. In this crisis moment of the church, many will find their own story in this book. Many of us will resonate with this longing to belong to something real and meaningful that points to the beauty and justice of God. This invitation to restoration through truth is one we all need."

—**Sandra María Van Opstal**, pastor and author of *The Next Worship*

"Pricelis Perreaux-Dominguez addresses the church with passionate love. Sometimes those with the strongest words speak boldly because they have ferocious hope. That hope is palpable through these pages. Pricelis calls the Body of Christ to rise up and shine like Christ himself."

—**Faith Eury Cho**, pastor and author of *Experiencing Friendship with God*

Being a Sanctuary

Being a Sanctuary

The Radical Way for the Body of Christ to Be Sacred, Soft & Safe

Pricelis Perreaux-Dominguez

BrazosPress
a division of Baker Publishing Group
Grand Rapids, Michigan

Published by Brazos Press
a division of Baker Publishing Group
Grand Rapids, Michigan
BrazosPress.com

Printed in the United States of America

Library of Congress Cataloging-in-Publication Data
Names: Perreaux-Dominguez, Pricelis, 1989– author.
Title: Being a sanctuary : the radical way for the body of Christ to be sacred, soft, and safe / Pricelis Perreaux-Dominguez.
Description: Grand Rapids, Michigan : Brazos Press, a division of Baker Publishing Group, [2024] | Includes bibliographical references.
Identifiers: LCCN 2024008559 | ISBN 9781587436413 (paperback) | ISBN 9781587436550 (casebound) | ISBN 9781493447961 (ebook)
Subjects: LCSH: Spiritual healing—Christianity.
Classification: LCC BT732.5 .P435 2024 | DDC 262.001/7—dc23/eng/20240326
LC record available at https://lccn.loc.gov/2024008559

The names and details of the people and situations described in this book have been changed or presented in composite form in order to ensure the privacy of those with whom the author has worked.

Cover illustration and typography by Erin Hung Studio

The author is represented by Alive Literary Agency, www.aliveliterary.com.

Baker Publishing Group publications use paper produced from sustainable forestry practices and postconsumer waste whenever possible.

24 25 26 27 28 29 30 7 6 5 4 3 2 1

To my husband,
Emanuel,
who has shown me *radical love*.

To my son,
Moses Peace,
who through my *radical labor*
made me a mama.

To my late father (may he rest in peace),
Luis Gustavo Perreaux Sr.,
who was the epitome of the fruits of the Spirit
seen through the *radical life* he lived.

And to you, the Body of Christ,
for picking up this book
and deciding that you love God
and others enough to be *sacred, soft, and safe*.

Contents

Introduction

(But, Really, an Invitation)

It's not a building you want to fill, it's my heart.
This empty space is what you wanted all along.
—Maverick City, "Come Again"[1]

It's no secret that the Body of Christ is in a crisis.

You, dear reader, might hear that and assume I'm trying to see only the bad. Other readers might affirm that statement to an unhealthy extent. My invitation to all of us is that we place ourselves between these extremes. Either end is extreme and not true. But what is true is that we indeed are in a crisis.

Throughout this book, I often share definitions of words, not just because I'm a writer but because we should define things as they are. *Crisis* is a word used in many different circumstances, so let's talk about its actual definition. According to the *Oxford English Dictionary*, *crisis* means:

- a time of intense difficulty, trouble, or danger
- a time when a difficult or important decision must be made

- the turning point of a disease when an important change takes place, indicating either recovery or death[2]

This is what I mean by crisis. We are in a time of intense difficulty within the Body of Christ. This certainly isn't the only time in history that the church has been in a crisis, but that doesn't mean we shouldn't do anything about it. We are experiencing intense division, scandals, people walking away from the faith, and dehumanization within the Body.

I like how the definition above takes us to a place of hope. A crisis is a time when an important or difficult decision needs to be made. So, a crisis is a time of difficulty but also a time to decide something. A crisis means something will either recover or die. In the case of the church, I think we need both.

There are things we believe, ways of being, and perspectives within the Body of Christ that really need to die. It's interesting that crisis means something needs to die because we are told we must die to ourselves in order to follow Jesus (Rom. 6:6). So perhaps a crisis is a sign to remember that truth.

I believe there's already much recovery happening within the Body of Christ right now, while there's also much recovery that is still needed in the areas of abuse, weariness, burned-out pastors, celebrity culture, scandals, misuse of money and power, division, racism . . . the list could go on.

It seems like we've been trying to figure all of this out on our own, but a crisis is an invitation for us to lean more into Christ. The Bible has answers. Church history has answers. Theologians and activists have answers. The Holy Spirit is our answer.

How do I know we *are* in a crisis?

In 2017, I realized it the most clearly when I left a church I worked for after experiencing spiritual abuse. While I knew things had been problematic for a while, I didn't realize to what extent until I left. I was on staff at a church that focused more on the Sunday service's lights and production than on what people needed outside its walls. I was given a code of silence the first day I began working there (more on that later) and was laughed at for being worried the day after Donald Trump was elected. I was silenced when I asked when I'd get sabbath rest. That's just the first church I worked for. The second one is a whole other story. The common thread between the two is that I didn't really know what it meant to be the Body of Christ—individually and collectively. That, friends, is a crisis because none of us should belong to the Body of Christ and not know how to be the Body of Christ.

In all my years in Christian spaces, I didn't actually learn what it meant to be the church. Instead, I learned bad theology about sabbath. I witnessed performative justice by a church that had the word *justice* in its mission statement. I saw people in dire circumstances ignored by pastors and other church staff. I saw marriages fall apart and families break. I saw people struggle with lust who had no one to guide them on how to be free. I saw person after person hurt, abused, wounded, forgotten, and traumatized within the church. I saw person after person "othered," discriminated against, and dehumanized within the church—a place that is supposed to be sacred, soft, and safe. And when I say "within the church," I don't mean a building or an organized Sunday service. I mean a gathering of people. These people aren't broken, but they are bruised and are bruising others. But we can praise God that nothing is so bruised that it can't be restored by his mighty hands.

The Radical Way of Christ

The radical way of Christ is not just a "God, heal us" road to restoration. No, this is a collaborative effort. Since we are his Body, we get to partner with God in rebuilding what has collapsed and healing what's been bruised. So here we are, in a battle for the restoration of the Body. For the found and the lost. For the good of the church and the glory of God. We are on a new path with old roots guiding us to be the Body—and be it well. But how do we get there?

Philippians 1:6 says, "He who began a good work in you will carry it on to completion until the day of Christ Jesus." We might read this and think, *Welp, I don't need to do anything about anything because God will complete the work*. But if we look at the history of God and his people, we see that God always includes people in active ways.

When he opened the Red Sea, the work of Israel was to walk through it.

When he sent Nehemiah as a leader, the work of Israel was to rebuild the city.

When he chose Mary, the work before her was to say yes and to raise a human being, fully divine and fully human.

When he sent Jesus, the work of the people was to repent, listen, believe, and follow.

When he blinded Paul, the work of Ananias was to help Paul understand his calling.

When he sent his Holy Spirit, the work of the church was to receive and listen to him.

There is always work to be done *with* God because we are his colaborers, as 1 Corinthians 3:9 says: "For we are coworkers in God's service; you are God's field, God's building."

God is using circumstances to create opportunities for us to work alongside him, to heal what has been bruised and redeem what has been misused. He will certainly continue and complete his work, but the way of the radical is to include ourselves in the story, to acknowledge that this is a collaborative effort.

What happens when we don't believe we play a part in healing the church?

We hold no responsibility.

We develop disconnection.

We become passive.

We miss the mission God has for us.

And we stop being the Body.

The Invitation

> Science may have found a cure for most evils; but it has found no remedy for the worst of them all—the apathy of human beings.
>
> —Helen Keller

Educator and advocate Helen Keller wasn't a Christian in any traditional sense, but her words are spot-on when it comes to considering how apathy is a dangerous road to walk, especially for those who claim to follow in the way of Jesus. We find ourselves in a difficult place of realizing that we've missed the radical invitation to live as the Body of Christ, deeply connected to one another, because our collective healing is integral to our individual healing. This is why apathy, passivity, division, and uniformity aren't the answers.

When we don't believe we have work to do in God's restorative plan, we hold no responsibility. This shows up in many ways, including a lack of repentance, accountability, and advocacy within the church and in the world. Instead, we must take responsibility, develop a connection to God's heart, renounce passivity, engage in the mission God has for the church, and be the Body.

When we don't believe we have work to do in God's restorative plan, we develop disconnection. This is dangerous because we can become legalistic (adhering excessively to law or rules, especially in the case of Scripture and Christian living), or we live so far beyond the roots of faith that Scripture holds no weight anymore. Or we become passive, cultural Christians with no connection to his church, or we simply consume Christian culture instead of contributing to building the healthy church.

When we don't believe we have work to do in God's restorative plan, we become passive. Passivity is a tool the enemy and his army use to keep Christians inactive regarding the injustice within the church and in the world.

When we don't believe we have work to do in God's restorative plan, we miss the mission God has for us. As the Body of Christ, we don't have separate missions. Our unified mission is found in Matthew 22:37–39: "Jesus replied: 'Love the Lord your God with all your heart and with all your soul and with all your mind.' This is the first and greatest commandment. And the second is like it: 'Love your neighbor as yourself.'" This is not only our mission but also a commandment. If we follow Christ, then living out his plan is something we will do intentionally, not occasionally or conditionally. This mission leads us to live out the Great Commission (Matt. 28:18–20).

Why does this matter? Why should we even care?

Friends, the church is at stake. Faith is at stake. The flourishing of those who bear the image of God is at stake. We can point fingers at one another and create long posts on Instagram about what's wrong with the church, but if we don't care enough to actually be part of the solution, then we are part of the problem.

Together in this book, we'll walk through what it looks like to be a Body of Christ that is Bible based (sacred), trauma informed (soft), and justice centered (safe). We will learn to prioritize Scripture, show compassion, and live justly in order for our churches, communities, and homes to be healthy, holy, humble, and helpful places that are considered sanctuaries once again.

There may be moments while you're reading this book when you get angry at or discouraged by the church's current state. You may also feel encouraged and hopeful. You might disagree with or get offended by some things I write. I hope all those feelings within you give you a deep understanding that in all of this we need Christ. We need him so we can see the truth, we need him to lead us to repentance, we need him to help us stay hopeful, and we need him so we can learn how to be the Body again. We get to join God in this good work.

God and his Word are essential for this process to actually bear good fruit and produce change. Because if it isn't good fruit, then we'll just remain in the same place we are now—disconnected, disoriented, and divided. On this journey, I hope we can grow in seeing our responsibility in all that's currently going on within the Body of Christ and develop a deep connection with these issues because this is a *whole-Body* concern. First Corinthians 12:26 says, "If one part suffers, every part suffers with it; if one part is honored, every part rejoices with it." We are one. Honored together and suffering together. We are currently suffering, but if we are willing, we can head in a new direction to become a sanctuary. A sanctuary is a safe place. A place of refuge. A place where people are protected. That is what and who we get to be as the Body—both to Christians and to the world. It is the radical way. It is Christ's way.

This Is for You

I think the fact that you picked up this book is a sign that you love the church and you want her to be restored and to move in a new direction. It also means you acknowledge the power of your actions, words, and life within the collective Body of Christ. We have the same goal, friend.

If you're a church member, may this book ignite a passion in you to be a part of the restorative work God is doing. You don't need to be an extrovert or consider yourself a leader to make changes toward healthy Christianity in your church and/or community. May these words also show you how you can grow personally in being the Body of Christ.

If you're a pastor, may this book convict you to reconsider approaches, structures, and perspectives that don't glorify God, aren't biblical, and aren't beneficial for your sheep. May these words also encourage you and make you feel seen in the ways that you have done your job well.

If you're on staff at a church, may this book help you see the weight of your position and how you can use your voice and authority to bring changes not just in your church but in the local churches around you and the churches in your denomination or church-planting network. May it also encourage you to see the beauty of what you can do as a staff member of a church.

If you don't go to church right now, may this book encourage you to know that people within the Body of Christ truly care about the state she is in and have deep hope in Christ that so much of what has been bruised and derailed can be restored and redeemed.

If you are looking for a new church, may this book be a blueprint for what to look for in a healthy church, may it help you not compromise where God wants to take you, and may it show you how you can contribute to the health of the Body.

If you're a Christian leader or have your own ministry, may this book take you on a journey of reflection to see where you perhaps have been a part of the problem and how you can be part of the solution. I hope it also encourages you in the areas you have been a part of in building the Body.

If you're a Christian, I hope this book reminds you that the Body is the church and the church is the Body and that our way of living, thinking, and communing comes not from a day of the week or a man-made structure but from a powerful God who had very good foundational plans for what the church would be and can still be.

Being the Body is not just good for the world; it also glorifies God and offers a restorative approach to living. When we are the Body, we exemplify compassion, dignity, justice, gentleness, grace, and all the things Jesus is. Being the Body is also not one person's call. Pastors are not responsible for the health of the collective church because they aren't the head; Jesus is. They, like you and me, are part of the Body of Christ and are responsible for helping it be sacred, soft, and safe. It's important we acknowledge this point because sometimes we hold pastors so responsible that we don't look at ourselves and how we have either contributed to the crisis or allowed the crisis to grow.

So let's get to work, and as we do, let's remember to hope in and rely on our sanctuary—Christ himself, who is "our refuge and strength, an ever-present help in trouble" (Ps. 46:1). We are indeed in trouble, but it's not too late for us. God is on our side. Glory hallelujah.

Things to Know before We Start

The point of the following summary is to share the goal of this book and the purpose behind each part of the book, what you'll find at the end of each chapter, and some things that were on my mind while I was writing.

The Goal

The goal of this book is to help the Body of Christ collectively reflect, repent, and move toward restoring the church to what God intended. My hope is that the church will process these words with intention, purpose, and action and leave with clarity and conviction, not confusion.

Three Sections of This Book

There are twelve chapters and three parts to this book. Each part has four chapters and a different purpose and topic.

Part 1: Sacred—From Passivity to Responsibility

This section explores being a Bible-based Body of Christ. It invites us to no longer choose passivity toward the way the Bible calls us to be the church and to move toward a place of responsibility for the work we need to do to restore health. It calls us to be sacred and to repent of the ways we've made church, our lives, and even our thinking world-based instead of Bible-based. It addresses church, Christian culture, sanctification, and Christian living. What I mean by *Bible-based* is that we are a people who learn from the descriptive parts of the Bible (stories of people and their interaction with God) *and* the prescriptive parts of the Bible (God's commandments and invitations to holiness).

Part 2: Soft—From Collision to Compassion

This part of the book addresses how we can be a trauma-informed Body of Christ. It explores trauma-informed care, being the church to the wounded, and unhealthy practices and attitudes the church is using that aren't trauma informed. It shows how we can move away from colliding with one another and toward being compassionate with one another and the world even amid differences. It addresses abuse, political stances, racism, and other areas we need to be softer in.

Part 3: Safe—From Observing to Responding

The final part of the book focuses on being a justice-centered Body of Christ. It examines what justice and injustice are, what the Bible says about them, how we can live justly, and why the topic of justice should matter to all Christians and not just to those who are "called" to justice work. This part shows that Jesus was not a mere observer of injustice but a responder to injustice and how we can be that too, daily and practically.

Moments to Selah

You'll also find in this book a prelude, two interludes, and a postlude. They are included as an invitation to selah in the form of prayer, poem, and Scripture. *Selah* is a word often found in the book of Psalms and other books of the Old Testament. It means to pause or to stop and listen. That, I believe, is God's consistent invitation to us. In a world full of so many voices, he's inviting us to stop and listen to his voice the most frequently and intentionally.

The prelude contains a Scripture passage I believe we should all study and reflect on often. We should never think that because we've read it before we don't need to read it again. It reveals what God calls us, and may we never forget who we are and the purpose we have here.

The first interlude appears after chapter 4. It's a response to a sermon I heard years ago by a pastor who gave his church a vision that is not aligned with the holy and humble Christ communicated in Scripture.

The second interlude is an invitation to meditate on Matthew 19:30 and what it means for our lives.

Finally, the postlude is a call to all of us. Just as a song has a beginning, middle, and end, so does the story of the collective church Body. No one knows for certain where we are in the story, but we do know that we get to leave a mark that is healthy and holy for future generations and every lost soul.

The End of Each Chapter

At the end of each chapter, you'll find four components: radical thoughts, reflective questions, restorative meditation, and remain in Scripture.

Radical thoughts. Here you'll find ideas based on the chapter. This is also the place for you to consider your own thoughts based on your reading.

Reflective questions. Answer these questions before you move on to the next chapter. Sit with them and maybe even discuss them with other people as a way to be an active participant in the work this book invites you to do.

Restorative meditation. Inhale and exhale as you meditate on the thoughts provided. These meditations are meant to be repeated a few times as an encouraging invitation to pray about what you just read.

Remain in Scripture. This section contains Scripture passages that were mentioned in the chapter or that I suggest you read in relation to the topics covered in the chapter. We should remain in Scripture, for Scripture holds the truth and shows us how to live the radical way of Jesus. It's what will guide us every time.

Sharing My Heart

Finally, these questions roamed my head as I was writing this book:

Will this be digestible for people?
Will people see me as an angry Black woman instead of someone who is passionate about building up the Body?
Will people see me as a Latina who wants a seat at the table instead of realizing that we should all be focused on building God's *casita* (house)?
Will I be seen as bitter because of my church wounds? Or will people choose empathy and see my deep love for the church and how the truth I share shows that?
Will my words change anything?

Most people probably don't have to ask these kinds of questions when writing a book. But I'm not most people. To many, I'm the minority. I'm the "other." I'm the token. I'm the hurt one. And that's also why I wrote this book: to give voice to those who've been silenced and who as vessels of the Spirit of the living God have a message to speak to his church.

So my prayer is that you'll read this book and see the words as Christ would see them: communicating a message of truth and grace, a message of accountability and compassion, a message of prevention and intervention, a message that convicts and does not conceal, a message from the heart of a woman who deeply loves the church and loves her enough to tell her the truth.

Colossians 3:12 says, "Therefore, as God's chosen people, holy and dearly loved, clothe yourselves with compassion, kindness, humility, gentleness, and patience." The Greek word for "compassion" is *oiktirmos*, and it indicates mercy or compassion toward people from the perspective of God. I pray that's how you'll read this book. That you will receive these words with empathy and have compassion for what I share but that they will also convict you and move you to act.

I started writing this book wanting to write something that was both digestible and true. My main goal ended up being just writing what is true, because if we can't digest the truth, that means we're just not ready for it. So my hope is that you build an appetite for and receive the Truth, because that is who Christ is. In Jesus's name, amen.

SELAH PRELUDE

Just as a body is one whole made up of many different parts, and all the different parts comprise the one body, so it is with the Anointed One. We were all ceremonially washed through baptism together into one body by one Spirit. *No matter our heritage*—Jew or Greek, insider or outsider—*no matter our status*—oppressed or free—we were all given the one Spirit to drink. *Here's what I mean:* the body is not made of one large part but of many *different parts.*

Would it seem right for the foot to cry, "I am not a hand, so I couldn't be part of this body"? Even if it did, it wouldn't be any less joined to the body. And what about an ear? If an ear started to whine, "I am not an eye; I shouldn't be attached to this body," in all its pouting, it is still part of the body.

Imagine the entire body as an eye. How would a giant eye be able to hear? And if the entire body were an ear, how would an ear be able to smell? *This is where God comes in.* God has meticulously put this body together; He placed each part in the exact place to perform the exact function He wanted. If all members were a single part, where would the body be?

So now, many members *function* within the one body. The eye cannot wail at the hand, "I have no need for you," nor could the head bellow at the feet, "I won't go one more step with you." It's actually the opposite. The members who seem to have the weaker functions are necessary to keep the body moving; the body parts that seem less important we treat as some of the most valuable; and those unfit, untamed, unpresentable members we treat with an even greater modesty. That's something the more presentable members don't need.

But God designed the body in such a way that greater significance is given to the *seemingly* insignificant part. That way there should be no division in the body; instead, all the parts mutually depend on and care for one another. If one part is suffering, then all the members suffer alongside it. If one member is honored, then all the members celebrate alongside it.

You are the body of the Anointed, *the Liberating King;* each and every one of you is a *vital* member.

—1 Corinthians 12:12–27 (The Voice)

PART 1

Sacred—From Passivity to Responsibility

Passivity may be the easy course, but it is hardly the honorable one.

—Noam Chomsky

1

Selah Will Be Our Saving Grace

The less I move, the more I know where God is.

—Common, "A Beautiful Chicago Kid"[1]

My sheep listen to my voice; I know them, and they follow me.

—John 10:27

It was a Sunday at 6:45 a.m. in 2016, 2017, or 2018—it's all a blur now. The day went by, and just like that it was 8:45 p.m. and I had eaten at most one meal. At that time, my husband was headed to his overnight shift at work, and I was headed home. We thought we were doing God's work.

In that season of our life and ministry, we didn't know how to live in silence, stopping, and stillness. It was simply not our normal way of living. Some people choose to meditate and be still, but our society is eager for rapid results and constant information. We see the inability to listen to God in the Bible too, so we don't need to feel so bad about moving so fast and not stopping to listen to God, right?

In the Psalms (and a few other books of the Bible), we find a beautiful word that is an invitation from God: selah. *Selah* is the Hebrew word that likely means "to stop and listen." In the context of Christian living, it's an invitation not just to pause but also to listen to God during the pause. The world's forms of meditating, reflecting, and thinking invite us to empty our minds and listen to our "inner self" or "inner truth." By contrast, selah means pausing to meditate on, reflect on, and think about what God is saying. We may not hear God audibly, but that doesn't mean he isn't speaking. Some hear him through a feeling. Others hear him through visions. All of us, if we follow Christ, have access to his voice, which we can find in the pages of Scripture. And because we can listen to him, we should do it. I know that may sound obvious and funny, but it's something many Christians aren't doing. I say that because of seeing the fruit of what many Christians are saying, thinking, and doing in the world.

We are a collective Body, which means we are responsible to one another. By way of the apostle Paul's words in 1 Corinthians 12, Christ says we are his Body. Where we currently are as a Body is dangerous. If we keep going, thinking we have the best practices and best approaches to "church," then we'll stay lost and keep hurting one another, and people will continue to walk away from the faith or not consider it at all.

We are speeding, and we need to selah instead.

I read a book the other day that said that, contrary to popular belief, Christianity isn't dying. The author stated this as a fact by pointing to statistics. I'm a big fan of data and numbers and believe they communicate information to help us as a society make wise decisions, yet when it comes to measuring the faith of followers of Christ, authentic faith can't be measured by polling data. Numbers don't tell us who is following Jesus—one's life does. If we were to look at the lives of the Christians we know and various public Christian leaders, we would at least wonder whether the Christian faith is expanding in a healthy way according to the Great Commission.

Matthew 28:19–20 says, "Therefore go and make disciples of all nations, baptizing them in the name of the Father and of the Son and of the Holy Spirit, and teaching them to obey everything I have commanded you. And surely I am with you always, to the very end of the age." There are no numbers in this passage, no call to make leaders, and no focus on one specific way of doing church. Instead, Jesus tells us to tell people the good news and form healthy communities that observe his commands.

How do we do this while we wait for Jesus to come back?

One of the best ways is through selah. To stop and listen. To stop and evaluate. To pause and reflect. To take a break and consider what is working and what isn't. To consider if what we are doing is biblical. To consider what is a priority and what isn't. To consider what is honorable and what is not dignifying. To consider what it is to be the Body of Christ while we are breathing this borrowed breath here on earth.

Selah as the Church

The Gospels include the following interaction between Jesus and Peter; it's the first time Jesus mentions "church" in the biblical accounts.

Matthew 16:15–16 says, "'But what about you?' he asked. 'Who do you say that I am?'" Simon Peter answers, "You are the Messiah, the Son of the living God." Jesus says, "Blessed are you, Simon son of Jonah, for this was not revealed to you by flesh and blood, but by my Father in heaven. And I tell you that you are Peter, and on this rock I will build my church" (vv. 17–18).

Peter had paused to listen to Jesus. When Jesus asks him a question, Peter has the answer, and his answer comes not from his flesh, knowledge, degrees, or experiences but from God. This is a moment of selah for Peter. He stopped and listened, and he responds with the truth, not his truth but God's truth—that's when the church began.

Since this is the way the church began, it should very well be the way the church continues.

Remember the story I told at the beginning of this chapter? The church I was busy working at is where I first learned the meaning of selah. Yet I wondered why it wasn't a word we applied in our culture and rhythms. Why weren't we teaching people to pause and listen to God? And, y'all, I live in New York City. If there's a group of people that needs to pause, it's New Yorkers. Like New Yorkers, some parts of the world of Christianity seem to be moving fast and not worrying about who is getting hurt on the path to "success" and "growth."

This church had two seasons of fasting a year like clockwork, yet I still didn't witness selah. We prayed at the beginning of each of our meetings, yet I saw no selah. We hosted services every week yet left no room for selah.

Here's the thing about selah: it's hard to do because it might mean we have to change how we do things based on what God says to us. Pausing and listening to God may mean we have to make less money or hold fewer services each week. It may mean we have to repent and apologize publicly for something. It may mean a pastor has to step down or an accountability meeting needs to happen. It may mean we have to renounce Christian celebrity culture, especially if we are in it, profiting from it, or perpetuating it. It may mean making difficult decisions we don't want to make. It may mean the church has to be a sanctuary and not a place where people are growing socially but not spiritually. It may mean abiding in God.

I get it. I surely avoid listening to God sometimes based on my assumptions of what he will say, because I want to follow my own emotions, or because I assume I will be convicted of something. So in many areas of my life, I keep going. But then I think about the cost. If I don't stop and listen or pause and reflect, how will it affect others? How will it affect my marriage and my son? How will it affect my family and my legacy? How will it affect those I serve and have helped before? How will it distance me from God or where he is leading me? These are questions to ask as we navigate selah, our emotions, and God's conviction.

I once heard someone say, "Our freedom is tied together." I would also say that much of our bondage and sin is tied together. This is what makes us a collective Body. We exist as many members of one Body. One of the many things that makes our faith distinct is that it's meant to be lived with others based on the example of Jesus with the disciples. God himself is three persons in one. Our suffering, issues, struggles, and challenges within the Body are collective. They are not just our own but something we all carry. Therefore, we need one another.

Choosing Selah to See

The church doesn't have a talking problem. She's saying plenty of things all the time. Instead, she has a listening problem. Notice the difference between talking and listening. Most people look around when they are talking. But when people are listening, they tend to look directly at the person talking and use eye contact. When we're listening, we are paying closer attention to the circumstance and the words being communicated. This is why taking time to selah as a spiritual practice is essential for Christians: it invites us to be better listeners to the voice of God and better listeners to a world that is suffering and struggling. Many people today would communicate that they feel the church is failing in several areas and that much of it has to do with what churches, church leaders, and Christians are saying and not saying.

The year 2020 was a wildly odd and traumatizing year for all of us. It included drastic changes we all had to make, and the church was not exempt. March 2020 hit, and churches that weren't already doing livestream services had to figure out a way to do them. Many faithful churches truly served their members and communities by addressing their traumatized state. But many other churches sent a loud message with no words. They were so focused on getting all the equipment and resources needed for livestream services that their congregations no longer were a priority. The priority was producing a service for people to watch when most of us just wanted someone to talk to, friends to connect with, answers on how to navigate this crisis with Christ at the center and not become bankrupt or evicted if we lost our jobs. There were huge needs, but some churches communicated that something else was more important: Sunday was more important. Perhaps Sunday was always more important to these churches, but it just didn't seem as obvious to us before then. (We'll get more into priorities as a church in chapter 2.) Our beloved sister Maya Angelou said, "When someone shows you who they are, believe them the first time."[2] The spring of 2020 helped us see our churches for who they really were. It was up to us after that to decide whether we would act like we hadn't seen it.

Then May 2020 came, and a beloved image bearer was murdered. Our brother George Floyd was sitting in his car after a store reported that he had used a counterfeit $20 bill. The cops approached him and dragged him out like he was an animal. He was on the street, handcuffed, and not resisting. And for nine minutes and twenty-nine seconds, police officer Derek Chauvin had his knee on Floyd's neck. Right here, let's take a moment to selah.

Inhale: Lord, we grieve the sin that is racism in this world.
Exhale: Holy Spirit, give us peace and comfort in this.

I remember not wanting to watch the video, but so many people were posting it that I couldn't avoid it. I eventually saw this dehumanization in action. This wasn't the first time a Black man was murdered this way in the United States of America. But something about it stirred up lots of people.

I remember getting apology texts from White friends and acquaintances and not really knowing how to feel. I remember the black boxes on Instagram, the protests, and churches led by White pastors inviting Black pastors to speak on this tragedy. But honestly, friends, what would have helped the most in the midst of the rage, disappointment, and pain was selah. That's what I believe could have shifted everything. For people to stop and listen—collectively. Many people at that time were saying to the Black community, "I'm listening," but what if those people had also stopped and listened to God? Our stories of experiencing trauma because of racism can motivate people only to a certain extent. We need God's Word to be our driving force for all things in life, including for justice.

People "listened" that summer, but when the noise died down, ears closed back up again. This is why our ultimate and most powerful selah needs to involve God. He knows and sees all, and because that's true, his truth will not waver through time. What was true about God two thousand years ago is still true. This is why choosing to stop and listen to him is essential.

When we listen to God, we see others. When we listen to God, we don't just pass that person on the street experiencing homelessness. When we listen to God, we show compassion before we judge someone. When we listen to God, we live a life of response instead of reaction. When we listen to God, we show up as the Body of Christ to the world differently. When we listen to God, we take responsibility. When we listen to God, our whole life changes, God is glorified, others are blessed, and the church is edified.

The Way of the Radical

If you're not familiar with the story of Moses, consider reading Exodus. In Exodus 14, Israel is walking in the desert after leaving the land where they were enslaved by Pharaoh, and they come upon the Red Sea. They see the Egyptians behind them ready to take them back to slavery, and as they are panicking, God tells Moses this in verse 16: "Raise your staff and stretch out your hand over the sea to divide the water so that the Israelites can go through the sea on dry ground." Moses does as God says, "and the Israelites went through the sea on dry ground, with a wall of water on their right and on their left" (v. 22).

As a church, we need to come back to the knowledge that God makes a way and that our role is to follow in that way. We contribute to what he's doing or wait on his timing, but either way we choose obedience. When we do not choose to selah, it's hard to follow God. It may even lead us to sin.

We, like Israel, are in a panic of sorts, and we need a Red Sea to part. But will we stop and listen to the God who gave the instruction in verse 16 so we can live in verse 22? Will we listen to the instruction of God and choose to obey it? Will we choose the way of the radical, a phrase we'll unpack throughout this book? When we walk in the way of the radical, we don't rely on our own independence and fundraising. When we walk in the way of the radical, we choose God's will over planned strategy. When we walk in the way of the radical, we are led not by our feelings but by faith in the one true God. When we walk in the way of the radical, we submit to what God has in mind even if it looks different from other churches.

The way of Jesus. The better way. The way of selah. The way of the radical. To be sanctuaries once again.

Perhaps we have lost the way, but there is no need to fear. Jesus knows the way. He will show us the path to follow. But we must be willing to stop and listen to him. Perhaps that's how we can go from being passive Christians to being the Body of Christ. That's what this first section of the book covers. Renouncing, denouncing, and even repenting of passivity and moving toward responsibility in order to be the sacred church God intended us to be.

Throughout this book, when I say "the Body," I'm usually talking about people, and when I say "the church," I'm usually talking about the collective and corporate gatherings that exist around the world under different denominations and leaders. This is an important distinction because restoring the church involves all of us relearning how to be the Body. This book isn't just about Sundays or one person's church. It's about all of us, collectively.

Let's change our selah deficiency and become a Body that delights in our silence and God's instruction. Let's become a Body that seeks out wise reevaluation, chooses repentance, reflects consistently, and wants to desperately represent Christ well.

Let's start here friends: take a deep breath as we selah through this Scripture that is a declaration and reminder of a God who is not silent but just, present, and righteous.

> The Mighty One, God, the LORD,
> Speaks and summons the earth
> from the rising of the sun to where it sets.
> From Zion, perfect in beauty,
> God shines forth.
> Our God comes
> and will not be silent;
> a fire devours before him,
> and around him a tempest rages.
> He summons the heavens above,
> and the earth, that he may judge his people:
> "Gather to me this consecrated people,
> who made a covenant with me by sacrifice."
> And the heavens proclaim his righteousness,
> for he is a God of justice. (Ps. 50:1–6)

May we listen to the One who is wise, and may we collectively rediscover the radical call to sacredness through the first section of this book.

RADICAL THOUGHTS

> Selah holds the answer to the rushing Christianity we are living in that seeks to fill seats but leaves souls empty.

> If we paused, we wouldn't get left behind but rather would move at the pace Christ designed for us, which is perfect and involves abiding in his will.

> Selah leads us to repentance. When we are always talking, there is no room to consider how we are sinning.

REFLECTIVE QUESTIONS

> When's the last time you stopped to listen to God without the prompting of a pastor or church service?

> How can you contribute to creating a culture of selah in your home, family, friend group, church, community, job, marriage, and life?

> What scares you about silence?

> What do you know about God's voice? What have you been taught about it, and what does the Bible say about it?

RESTORATIVE MEDITATION

INHALE: Lord, I'm here to listen.

EXHALE: I repent of all the times I bypassed your voice to amplify my own.

INHALE: I am here to be a part of your Body on earth in a way that is healthy and whole.

EXHALE: Show me everything that is getting in the way of me being able to do and be that.

INHALE: Your voice, mission, and church matter more than . . .

EXHALE: my goals, the analytics, and what other Christians have said success is.

REMAIN IN SCRIPTURE

- o Exodus 14
- o Psalm 50:1–6
- o Matthew 16:15–18
- o Matthew 28:19–20
- o John 10:27
- o 1 Corinthians 12
- o Ephesians 5:22–33

2

Higher and Holier

I look at my environment
And wonder where the fire went

—Lauryn Hill, "The Miseducation of Lauryn Hill"[1]

For I have come down from heaven not to do my own will but to do the will of him who sent me.

—John 6:38

If the apostle Paul were to write a letter to the church in the United States, what would he write? Most of his letters (the epistles of the New Testament) include correction, conviction, compassion, and some congratulations. If you have social media, then you may have seen the viral video of someone pretending to be Paul writing a letter to the church in the United States. The video creator starts the letter by saying, "To the church in

America, it ain't looking good."[2] Although I chuckled when I saw that, the words hold deep truth that may lead us to a conviction or two.

When Paul wrote his letters that compose much of the New Testament, he wasn't talking to a building or the staff at a church. He wasn't always talking only to those who claimed to follow Jesus in a particular city. This matters because often our sins, shortcomings, and challenges aren't ours alone but things we share with others and that affect others. This book is not meant to be read and processed alone, just like the Christian walk is not meant to be done alone, just like our engagement with God's Word is not meant to be done alone (although alone time in it is important). We experience sins, shortcomings, and challenges as a Body, not just individually.

This book is titled *Being a Sanctuary* because this faith of ours is a collective one. Jesus didn't have to call us his Body. He could have just said, "You're my bride" and "You're my church," but he specifically called us his Body too. Paul writes this in one of his letters to the church in Corinth:

> The eye cannot say to the hand, "I don't need you!" And the head cannot say to the feet, "I don't need you!" On the contrary, those parts of the body that seem to be weaker are indispensable, and the parts that we think are less honorable we treat with special honor. And the parts that are unpresentable are treated with special modesty, while our presentable parts need no special treatment. But God has put the body together, giving greater honor to the parts that lacked it, so that there should be no division in the body, but that its parts should have equal concern for each other. If one part suffers, every part suffers with it; if one part is honored, every part rejoices with it. (1 Cor. 12:21–26)

This is what a sanctuary is in God's eyes: a place where people know the purpose of the Body.

A place where people are willing to suffer together.
A place where people gladly rejoice together.
A place where people know they need each other.
A place where people honor all parts of the Body and where division is not seen.

A sanctuary is not something we have to become because God has already designed us to be a sanctuary. It's what God formed us to be. Being a sanctuary is something we get to choose to be. Sanctuaries are sacred, soft, and safe places and people.

- Sanctuaries are sacred by holding to God's biblical truth in a way that glorifies him and edifies the Body.
- Sanctuaries are soft by putting people and their stories above opinion and stance.
- Sanctuaries are safe by living justly and acknowledging the belovedness in every person God has formed.
- Sanctuaries are radical followers of Jesus willing to be responsible with God's Word, compassionate with others, and responders to injustice.

This is not just a calling. It's the way of Jesus, and one we agreed to be a part of when we said yes to him. The purpose of this book is to offer guidance on how to be sanctuaries once again. To show how we have departed from the radical way of Jesus and how we can return to being a devoted and integrity-filled Body. So if we can imagine getting a letter from the apostle Paul, it would read something else besides "it ain't looking good."

A City on a Hill

Matthew 5 tells us that we are called to be a city on a hill shining the light of Jesus. But the light some of us are shining is basically an ad for our Sunday services, our next program, our opinions, and the celebrity pastors we love. It's not the light of Jesus but a superficial light that must be turned off.

Our response to the gift of salvation should be aligning ourselves with Christ. This means his priorities are ours. Jesus doesn't leave us here trying to guess what his priorities are; he made them clear through his Word and his life. But somehow many of us have misinterpreted them.

Let's start with one of the most obvious and important priorities of Jesus: love. John 13:34–35 says, "A new command I give you: Love one another. As I have loved you, so you must love one another. By this everyone will know that you are my disciples, if you love one another." He also says this in Matthew 22:37 but includes loving God, which is a reference to Deuteronomy 6:5. Now some of you may be thinking, I can skip to the next page or chapter because I've got love covered. I can understand why you may feel or think this way, but please stick around.

Love is one of the most complex feelings and choices in the world because it's so overused in media, marketing, and movies that we may not even realize how we are mixing up God's way of love with the world's way. God's way of love is less about fluffy things, romance, and being nice to people. God's love is displayed most clearly and powerfully on the cross. And what does the cross mean? Salvation and liberation for all. But what did it cost? Sacrifice and pain. Because Jesus said, "Just as I have loved you, you are also to love one another," there must be a more practical way to love as the Body of Christ who has experienced God's love firsthand.

Loving Our Churches

If you follow me on Instagram or subscribe to my Substack, then you know I'm not quiet about calling out the characteristics of an unhealthy church. While some assume I talk about such things because I am bitter or haven't healed, they are wrong. I call out these things because I love the church and want to see her be healthy and whole. If you love your friend and they are continually sinning, don't you say something to them? Is being silent really loving them? Rather than shaming them or belittling them, we call our friends to something higher and holier. That's love because that's exactly how Christ loves us. He calls us to something higher and holier. If we look at stories in the Gospels, we notice a pattern of Jesus loving people by healing them and calling them away from sin and to him. He tells them to sin no more, not in a shameful or hurtful way but in a loving and direct way. We'll get into how trauma informed Jesus was in the second part of this book, but for now, we get to learn from our dear friend Jesus how to love people well.

Who is in our churches? People. Loving the church means we live out Isaiah 1:17: "Learn to do right; seek justice. Defend the oppressed. Take up the cause of the fatherless; plead the case of the widow."

People are so scared to say there's a problem with the church. I've concluded this is because

they feel it will discount or diminish the good the church has done; and

fixing the church will require work and change and probably some repentance (personally and/or collectively).

But we get to live by the words of Isaiah 1:17 and learn what is good for others, the church, and the world. We get to learn what is not good and be a part of restoring things back to good. As Isaiah 1:17 reminds us, we can be so focused on church programs and Sunday services that we forget the essentials and basics of what God has called us to as the Body of Christ Monday through Saturday.

In *When Church Stops Working*, Andrew Root and Blair D. Bertrand state, "Let's start with the bad news. Your church is sick. But that isn't the worst part of it. We believe that someone has misdiagnosed it. The treatment plan commonly prescribed—effective innovation—will only cause your church to remain sick. The good news is that your church can get healthy, though it won't be easy."[3] The church, as a Body, can have ailments, get sick, and be misdiagnosed. Imagine if we ignored those things in regard to our own bodies. Would that be loving or honoring the bodies God has given us? Then the same applies to how we respond to abuse, racism, division, trauma, misuse of God's Word, and dehumanization within the Body of Christ. We acknowledge that there's bad news to pay attention to while loving the Body enough to want it to be healthy again. As Root and Bertrand note, healing the church won't be easy, but we haven't chosen the easy route. We've chosen the path that leads us to be sanctuaries—not just for the people in our churches and families but for every image bearer on earth.

Loving Our Pastors

Something that people often miss when I talk about religious trauma and church abuse is that I'm talking about pastors who are wounded too. When we decide that pastors are the bad guys, we center our perspective on scandals. But the truth is that there are many faithful pastors around the world—shepherds who understand the call to protect and lead the sheep they have been assigned. Loving our pastors is an essential part of exemplifying love in the world. They are sinners, just like us, and struggle with difficult things, just like us. They have a mantle that isn't ours to carry, but we can love them well by interceding for them and loving them.

Loving them sometimes also means confronting them. We belonged to a church a while back whose pastor was unhealthy. He was growing an ego, and the church was slowly but surely becoming all about him. He lacked accountability, with no elders, pastors, or bosses above him. When we decided to leave the church, several others left as well. We left because of a major issue that came up within that community in that season, but it was never resolved, because the ones who stayed didn't say anything. That is not loving. When we set out to love our churches, we also ought to love our pastors. At one point the pastor said, "No church or person is perfect, but we try." Later, he stepped down due to moral failure.

The pastor was right about one thing: no church or person is perfect. But the response should not be "let's just keep going." It should be "let's slow down, repent, and reevaluate." That's loving a congregation, the church, and the call we've been given by God.

Here's what love isn't. A well-known pastor committed a sin against his wife and his church a few years ago. It ended up in the news. He wrote a social media post admitting what he had done (partially) and apologizing. Immediately, the comments section was flooded with messages like "I love you," "We love you," and "We support you no matter what." Most of the people commenting did not personally know this pastor. Am I saying it's wrong to say "I love you" to people who have fallen? No. What I'm saying is that often people are convicted by both the Holy Spirit and the godly counsel and words of people around them. The pastor later showed up in a documentary series in which he admitted to what he had done to his wife but still denied something he had done to another woman who was a former employee. He disappeared and stepped down, but he did not repent for all he had done. He also blamed his own pastor for "molding him" in this way.

As the Body of Christ, we love this person because he is an image bearer of God. But loving him is not necessarily telling him we love him superficially on a comments thread. Rather, it's holding him accountable. Often people hear the word *accountable* and think of cancellation. But in the kingdom of God, there's no such thing. There is, however, repentance and redemption.

To love our pastors is to extend them grace, communicate truth to them, pray for them often, and invite them to something higher and holier.

Loving Our Enemies and People We Disagree With

Friends, much of the church is struggling with loving people we disagree with. If you weren't a Christian and you read posts and comments by Christians on social media, you might be confused because they don't sound like Christ. A friend of mine says this all the time: "Jesus looks at the comments section too, so check yourself." We have misinterpreted disagreement and made it mean that we can dehumanize, disrespect, and dishonor. This is especially the case on social media, where we try to argue with someone we don't know, expecting them to be convinced by our rude or passive-aggressive commentary. But loving those who hate us and those we disagree with is an essential part of the restorative work God is doing in the world—creating a higher and holier Body of Christ. We'll touch on tangible examples of this later in the book, but I wanted to mention it here because it's a priority Jesus both displayed and commanded. Love others as yourself.

Loving the Wounded

The number of people who shame, condemn, other, ignore, and disregard those who have been wounded within the church is astounding and disappointing. It's not the way of the radical. It's the way of disconnecting ourselves from empathy and dismissing people's trauma, as if being harmed by the very people who are supposed to be the safest in the world is something we can just accept. Wounded people, in general, need us to be higher and holier because they're struggling to be anything but miserable. Loving them is helping them carry their cross, just like Simon of Cyrene did when he helped the wounded Jesus carry the cross he would be crucified on. In the case of Simon, he was forced to carry Jesus's cross (Luke 23:26). Instead of feeling forced, we do it willingly for the wounded because it's the higher and holier way.

Following and Leading

One of Jesus's priorities during his earthly ministry was teaching us who to follow and how to follow them. Jesus invites us, by way of Paul's letter to the church in Philippi, to walk humbly: "In your relationships with one another, have the same mindset as Christ Jesus: Who, being in very nature God, did not consider equality with God something to be used to his own advantage; rather, he made himself nothing by taking the very nature of a servant, being made in human likeness. And being found in appearance as a man, he humbled himself by becoming obedient to death—even death on a cross!" (Phil. 2:5–8).

Jesus shows that humility is one of the most important elements not only of leadership but also of being a Christian. He, who was and is God, didn't use that identity to exploit, abuse, or use people. He used it to help, fight for, love, and save people. Is humility a characteristic we look for in those we follow and allow to pastor us? It should be. Jesus displayed humility in all of his ministry, especially on the cross.

The other day a leader asked people online, "What have you experienced to be good and bad leadership? To be healthy and life-giving leadership? To be unhealthy and abusive?" This leader has made himself a safe, humble, and trustworthy leader, so people responded and shared their opinions and stories. This reminds me of Jesus. Everyone who encountered him was brutally honest, and I believe it's because they felt safe with him and trusted that he would hold their stories sacred. The call to be a higher and holier pastor or Christian leader is this: to be humble, teachable, safe, curious, and consistent.

I once had a pastor who was the opposite of this. We were around the same age, and this was his first official job (that in and of itself was problematic). He seemed to feel that he had all the answers. Some of the most dangerous people on earth are those who feel they have arrived. As Christians, we can be confident that we have the answer, which is Jesus, but if we aren't careful, all other knowledge outside of that truth can come from a place of ego, pride, or arrogance. I am currently in seminary and have two master's degrees. Technically, when you have a master's degree, you're a master at something (at least in academia). But I can tell you right now that I am not a master of anything. I am but a humble servant who acknowledges that I will be learning and unlearning for the rest of my life. The gifts and skills I've been given have been by the grace of God. This mindset isn't just healthy. It's one that creates room for people to feel safe, seen, and supported. It places us next to people instead of in front of them or above them. Even Jesus, someone who literally knows it all and is God himself, didn't let that make him unapproachable, arrogant, or boastful.

Last year I watched the movie *Honk for Jesus. Save Your Soul.* and recently I rewatched it. It's about a fallen pastor and his wife trying to relaunch their church after a scandal that involved the pastor manipulating, using, and sexually involving himself with young men in his church. The pastor and his wife want to re-launch the church on Easter Sunday but face several challenges along the way. Unfortunately, the dynamics of the story mirror real stories of Christians, pastors, and churches.

In the movie, the pastor tries to convince himself and others that because he's done good, his evil deeds can be overlooked. But when we repent and ask God for forgiveness, we don't mention the good deeds we did that day or the past week. So why do we do this with other people? Sin requires repentance, and sin against others requires a bigger and longer process of apologizing, learning, and processing. Sin is sin. Repentance is not a conversation about our worth or goodness.

Tim Holmes, the pastor I mentioned earlier who asked questions about leadership, went on to write a sermon in which he said, "Pastors shouldn't focus on protecting themselves or perpetrators in the church but instead protect the poor and vulnerable." If you're looking for a healthy pastor or Christian leader who is committed to a higher and holier way, this is what you should be looking for.

Part of leadership involves discipleship. The churches where I've worked revered leadership as the ultimate way to be a Christian and gave discipleship a back seat. There was no discipleship structure or even talk of discipleship. The focus was on growth, gifts, and leadership development. Can discipleship come from leadership development? For sure. But if the teaching is not structured to be discipleship, then the development will be centered on leadership.

I asked pastors in both those churches to disciple my husband. I got so many no's. It was exhausting and disheartening. Discipleship was just simply not their priority. This is not a unique experience. I have had many conversations with friends who asked or hoped for the same from their pastors and were told no. I've heard something similar from people struggling with sins and wanting support, direction, or accountability. Their pastors and ministry leaders simply do not have the time. As someone who has worked for a church, I have seen behind the scenes. There are certainly a lot of things pastors "have to do," but this is why we can't rely on one specific leader for discipleship. We certainly don't rely on just one leader for leadership development. It's often the leaders of the church who are developing the members of the church, and these members can disciple and pastor. The priority is then character development over leadership and gifts development. What good is a gift if the person is living in a constant sin struggle that is leading them to depression or overcompensation?

Partiality

I'm really boggled by this one. Partiality is one of those topics that not one person on earth can say the Bible isn't clear on it. The majority of Jesus's ministry was focused on dismantling division, seeing the overlooked, eating with those who were considered sinners, and choosing twelve disciples who were regular people. He holds no partiality with anyone, yet we struggle to do this. There are people whose voices and messages we amplify while others we ignore. Jesus's beloved brother teaches us about partiality in James 2:1–5:

> My brothers and sisters, believers in our glorious Lord Jesus Christ must not show favoritism. Suppose a man comes into your meeting wearing a gold ring and fine clothes, and a poor man in filthy old clothes also comes in. If you show special attention to the man wearing fine clothes and say, "Here's a good seat for you," but say to the poor man, "You stand there" or "Sit on the floor by my feet," have you not discriminated among yourselves and become judges with evil thoughts? Listen, my dear brothers and sisters: Has not God chosen those who are poor in the eyes of the world to be rich in faith and to inherit the kingdom he promised those who love him?

One of the most beautiful things about the Christian faith is that it's for everyone. The fact that socioeconomic, racial, gender, and theological differences within the Body of Christ create partiality among us is something we should take more seriously than we do. If we look at it biblically, partiality is dehumanizing. It runs counter to the cross. It's saying some have VIP access and others don't for various reasons. This is unbiblical, dishonorable, and not holy. In much of the contemporary church, Jesus himself would be treated poorly for his relationship status (unmarried), socioeconomic status (not wealthy), what he wore, whom he hung out with, and how he lived. Would he be welcome in our churches? Would we buy his books? Would he even get a publishing deal? Would he be invited to speak at conferences? Would he be served if seen on the street? In the third part of this book, we discuss how partiality is a justice and dignity issue and how we can look at it practically as we consider how Jesus's priorities included showing dignity to people and how partiality diminishes that.

The Bible

Probably one of the most misinterpreted books in the world is the Bible. It contains imagery and metaphors as well as literal teachings and descriptions. It consists of prescriptive verses that teach us how to be Christians and descriptive verses that tell us the history of God's people and his redemptive plan. It's made up of various genres and even genres within those genres, and amid all of that it communicates God's heart. It shows us who he is and his vision for the world. It tells us how loved we are. It's the story of God creating, redeeming, and restoring humanity.

But the text has been misinterpreted, misused, and misunderstood. I know we love to go to God's Word mainly for a word, encouragement, and answers, but God meant for it to guide, correct, convict, and teach us too (2 Tim. 3:16). Jesus himself showed us how important it is by quoting the Old Testament when engaging in conversations with people and teaching them. One of the ways we have not made the Bible our priority is by misusing it. I see this show up in three ways.

Bias. We project our stories and ourselves onto the biblical text. Our identities were formed by God, so they hold importance for who we are and how we navigate the world, but it's essential that we not add something to Scripture that simply isn't there. That's what our bias sometimes does. We read the Bible through our experiences, opinions, perspectives, and even traumas while dismissing the historical or cultural context. I am a married, Black, Latina woman, and Jesus was a single, Jewish man. Identity-wise, we don't have many similarities, but I don't need to relate to my Savior to love him, receive his salvation, and learn from him. Within my community, some people say, "My Jesus is Black," just like some people said, "My president is Black" when Obama won. Jesus is certainly not White—as so many books and paintings have portrayed him to be—but neither is he Black. He made me in his image; I don't need to make him in mine. When I do, I'm telling a different story. When I don't make him in my image, I don't project my Black or Latina experience onto his Jewish one.

Are there similarities to our experiences? Absolutely. Jesus came from a marginalized people, didn't grow up wealthy, and had to deal with oppressors and religious people. That has certainly been my experience, as it has been for many. I can preach sermons based on womanhood and injustice in the Bible that perhaps a man or a more privileged person can't. My context matters in the story of God, but that doesn't mean I have to put my context into every story or teaching.

Biblical illiteracy. Seminary has shown me why people struggle to understand the Bible: it is not an easy book to read. The church can certainly get better at both teaching the Bible and learning how to study it. We quote passages out of context and do devotions based on quick consumption of the Bible. We do not prioritize the Bible, and this affects how we are the Body of Christ, how we communicate, and how we live. If we don't read the Bible well, how will we follow Jesus well? What we have learned to do well is listen to how others read and interpret the Bible, but our engagement with God's Word cannot be based solely on what others say about it. There are many unorthodox and unbiblical theologies out there, and God already warns us that, if we are not careful, we will hear only what we want to hear:

> For the time will come when people will not put up with sound doctrine. Instead, to suit their own desires, they will gather around them a great number of teachers to say what their itching ears want to hear. (2 Tim. 4:3)

I'll be honest, I struggle to read some things in the Bible because of my context and gender and the century I'm living in. But none of that should trump the truth of God's Word. Even when I wrestle with the truths that exist in the Bible, I still get to remember God's heart. But I can know God's heart only by—you guessed it—reading the Bible.

What's encouraging to see is the response to false teachings, motivational speaking sermons, and surface-level "Bible" teaching: in response, churches, ministries, and Bible teachers are creating programs, resources, books, and spaces for people to learn theology and grow in the Word. Talk about some good ol' discipleship. I'm here for it!

Consumer culture. We live in a time of information. For everything we could possibly ask on Google, we can find not just one answer but numerous ones. We can learn about breaking news and global events more quickly than any people in history. Social media gives us access to people in a way that humans never did before. But what has all of this information done? It's caused us to become consumers. We watch thirty-second sermon clips on YouTube or read a five-slide carousel on Instagram or listen to a twenty-minute podcast episode. But what do we do with this information? How do we process it? Do we take time to investigate whether the information is true or valid? Do we take a few minutes to pray about or process the thirty-second sermon clip before we keep scrolling? Do we apply any of the tips shared on the podcast episode? The same is true in church and other Christian spaces too. We attend Sunday services, buy Christian books, and binge Christian content, but do we take the time to process any of it? Or is it just sitting in our brains? Are we perhaps doing this with the Bible too?

Jesus shows us another way. We don't know much about the life of Jesus between his early teen years and his early thirties, but based on the life he lived in his thirties, we can deduce that he spent a good amount of time in the Word of God. He didn't rush through it or just take it in as information. When he began his ministry, it was evident, not just because of what he said (when reciting the Old Testament) but also because of how he lived, that he had been with God (as God) and that he had spent time studying the Old Testament. We'll talk about this in numerous ways throughout this book: how we live is a true testament of what we know and think about God as well as how we are connected to him.

Justice

We will touch on justice further in part 3 of this book, but I want to mention it here because we have completely disconnected justice from Jesus. We leave the work of justice to the social workers and activists, but justice is a priority for Jesus. That means it should be a priority for every person who claims to follow him. Paul closes the book of Titus with these final remarks: "Our people must learn to devote themselves to doing what is good, in order to provide for urgent needs and not live unproductive lives" (Titus 3:14). The phrase "learn to devote" suggests taking time to do something—we learn something only by doing it for an extended period of time. And notice the last part of that sentence: "provide for urgent needs." Our time on earth is fleeting (Ps. 39:4), and we are to commit our time to doing good and providing for urgent needs, not being unproductive. That message is communicated throughout the Bible, especially in the Old Testament, and we see a similar statement in the New Testament by Jesus's brother, James: "Religion that God our Father accepts as pure and faultless is this: to look after orphans and widows in their distress and to keep oneself from being polluted by the world" (James 1:27). The Christian life looks like this: caring for the overlooked and marginalized.

This is the work of justice. Jesus prioritized this work in who he walked with, ministered to, fought for, healed, and listened to. Justice and the church are not separate departments of Christianity. The Body of Christ is called to prioritize justice in all ways. Absent justice, we are living a partial Christian walk and disobeying what God has commanded of us (read Isaiah 1!).

If we are a people who live connected to God, then our lives will display a higher and holier picture of something beyond us. Much of what Jesus teaches us is how to be like him. He is a high being and holy God, and how he showed up in the world made a huge difference. Women were seen and treated differently after his earthly ministry. The marginalized were seen and treated differently after his earthly ministry. The Gentiles and lepers were seen and treated differently after his earthly ministry. What does this tell us? Because Jesus lived out the will of the Father, things changed. If we, the Body of Christ, were to make his priorities our priorities, then we too would live out the will of the Father. We would live higher and holier lives. Not unto us or for our own glory. Not to become our "best selves" or to live our "best lives." But because the world (including us) is in deep need of another way. The way of the radical.

We can't honestly say we don't know Jesus's priorities—I've laid out a few in this chapter (obviously not all of them). If we were to selah and reflect, we would see that much of what we've prioritized in the modern faith is not fully aligned with Jesus's priorities. He's calling us to live a life that requires higher and holier thinking, decisions, communication, and approaches that honor humanity and give him glory. Higher doesn't mean we are above anyone; it means we do things to fulfill Matthew 6:10: "Your kingdom come, your will be done, on earth as it is in heaven." His will and not ours. And holier is explained in 1 Peter 1:15–16: "But just as he who called you is holy, so be holy in all you do; for it is written: 'Be holy, because I am holy.'"

We can no longer excuse ourselves by saying we don't know God's priorities. Instead, we can choose to follow the messianic radical who has called us to higher and holier ways.

RADICAL THOUGHTS

> Biblical examples show what our churches should and could be.

> Every person is a leader and holds influence where they are.

> Loving others includes correction and compassion.

> Misinterpreting the Bible comes at a cost.

> Your enemy is still your neighbor.

REFLECTIVE QUESTIONS

> When's the last time you reflected on the purpose of some of the things your church does on Sundays or as a collective organized group?

> How do you view your pastor or leaders? If they were to fall, how would you be Christlike to them or the situation?

> How do you grow in your biblical understanding? Do you rely on others and their interpretations, or have you sought out tools to help you grow in this area?

> How have you loved the church well?

> How do you practically live a higher and holier life?

RESTORATIVE MEDITATION

INHALE: Jesus, we thank you for showing us the way.

EXHALE: Forgive us for not always following it.

INHALE: God, we thank you for your patience and grace toward the church.

EXHALE: Holy Spirit, we ask that you continue to convict us as you call us to a higher and holier life.

INHALE: Jesus, leader of our church,

EXHALE: humble us.

REMAIN IN SCRIPTURE

- o Deuteronomy 6:5
- o Isaiah 1:17
- o Matthew 5:14
- o Matthew 6:10
- o Matthew 22:37
- o Luke 23:26
- o John 6:38
- o John 13:34–35
- o John 15
- o Acts 2:42
- o 1 Corinthians 12:21–26
- o Philippians 2:5–8
- o James 2:1–13
- o 1 Peter 1:15–16

3

The Roots of Uniformity and the Road toward Unity

> We are each other's harvest: we are each other's business: we are each other's magnitude and bond.
>
> —Gwendolyn Brooks[1]

> My prayer is not for them alone. I pray also for those who will believe in me through their message, that all of them may be one, Father, just as you are in me and I am in you. May they also be in us so that the world may believe that you have sent me.
>
> —John 17:20–21

As I'm writing this chapter, I'm in Seattle, drinking a flat white with oat milk at a Starbucks. Serious coffee drinkers who despise

Starbucks, please don't judge me. As I sit here waiting for a friend, I can't help feeling like I'm back home in New York City because the colors, font, menu, culture, tone, playlist, and prices are just the same as they are in Starbucks in New York City. Nothing is different but the state I am in. As the kids would say, it's the same vibe.

This is what businesses do, and it's a smart practice because it's about branding, consistency, and financial growth. I have been to thirty-three countries in the world and about twenty states, and in almost all of them I've seen a Starbucks that has mainly looked the same as all the others.

For many people, this is what they want and think the church should be, and in many ways, yes, we should be the same in our beliefs and Christlike character. Christians around the world should be known for how they display love, are generous, serve, and spread kindness. But this shouldn't be the case for how Christians dress, talk, think, worship, and live. Yet in many ways and places, we have adopted a mainstream majority culture that expects all Christians to be the same. This is the root of church trauma and abuse, it's the root of church scandals and pastors stepping out of their marriages, it's the root of people being turned off by the church. It isn't the only root for these things, nor is it the only reason why these things occur, but it certainly plays a part in what we have made the church to be.

If you visit a church in the United States (especially a church plant or a megachurch), you may notice how people seem to dress and talk similarly to people in other churches you've been to. Many churches, not just in the United States, have developed the Starbucks model. This is the idea that a church should look and sound like other churches to be successful, seem relevant, and be considered a welcoming or cool place to be. But this is far from what we see in the Bible when it comes to how the Body of Christ gets to think, act, speak, and live. We, the Body of Christ, aren't meant to be replicas of one another. We are to reject uniformity and live in the uniqueness that God has given us.

The church is not a business or a brand but a place and a people who are meant to look like and follow Jesus. The Starbucks model limits our ability to do this. The Starbucks model for churches communicates the following things:

- Language: we should all speak in "Christianese," especially using phrases like "do life together," "that's so good," "you belong before you believe," "I want to honor you," "Can I encourage you?" and so on.
- Attire: hip, urban attire. (When I was growing up in the church in the 1990s, we wore our Sunday best and my brothers couldn't wear hats in church. The dress code is not as strict now, but it still feels uniform in some ways.)
- Church format/focus: teams and not ministries, leadership development over discipleship, lots of lights on stage that are moving throughout the service, and so on.

Asking "Can I encourage you?" isn't inherently bad. But uniformity in language can create Christians who sound the same despite their unique settings, cultural backgrounds, languages, contexts, and outreach to nonbelievers. I live in the Bronx—and ain't nobody saying "Can I encourage you?" as a way to speak life into someone. So if I'm a church planter in the Bronx talking this way, I will lose the local people because that's not how they talk. Rather, I will attract other people who talk like that—meaning other Christians from *other* places, which amplifies the process of gentrification. And when I talk that way, many others in the church community start talking that way too, even if it's not natural based on geography and cultural context. The Starbucks model of language affects a church's evangelism, uniqueness, identity, mutuality, and honor in a local neighborhood.

Without even realizing it, over time at my first church position, I began to change how I dressed. I slowly began to dress like them and I began to talk like them. This is how uniformity works—even with something that seems so simple like attire. It starts there and evolves.

What I hope you see in these examples is that the church is focused on being monolithic instead of being monotheistic. The monolithic standard from Christianity's earliest days in the United States is White in culture and norm and male dominated—and it's certainly reaching its goal.

When Martin Luther King Jr. said, "I think it is one of the tragedies of our nation—one of the shameful tragedies—that 11 o'clock on Sunday morning is one of the most segregated hours, if not the most segregated hour, in Christian America,"[2] he was addressing three things: segregation, safety, and self.

Segregation in our churches is still very much a thing, and it goes beyond race. It shows up in a separation of theologies, age ranges, disabilities, socioeconomic statuses, and celebrity cultures. Some churches are committed to being multicultural and intergenerational, which is a beautiful thing. But this shouldn't be the commitment of a few churches. It should be the narrative of all churches. There are certainly some towns in the United States that have more people from one racial group than another or from one socioeconomic class than another. We can't force or expect that in some places, but diversity (in all senses of the word) should be the norm in churches.

The division in King's day was tragic, tragic because of the separation but also tragic because both sides of the racial divide in the United States didn't feel safe being in one space together. The Black people probably didn't feel safe because at that time whenever Black people showed up where White people were, often Black people ended up getting shot, arrested, or discriminated against. And White people probably didn't feel safe to share a space with Black people because of the narrative many of them believed about Black people.

"Self" was one of the reasons for this tragedy of division because people were looking out for themselves more than dignifying others and glorifying God. They chose to be comfortable rather than Christian. They chose to feel a superficial safety rather than create a sacred space for all image bearers to be, grow, and glorify God.

Churches largely remain segregated for the same reasons as before, but the safety element has changed. Some people don't feel safe going to church because they've been abused by someone in a church or because they don't feel welcome. We don't welcome people as they are, even though most churches say, "Come as you are." We want people to talk, act, think, and live a certain way—still the way of the majority: culturally White and with the central focus on men, even though women make up the majority of the church. This is the Starbucks church model: we should be one brand, uniform for God's glory.

The Church Model We've Idolized

A few years ago, an old pastor of mine called me and apologized for how they behaved with me in part because they were so focused on mimicking Hillsong back then. Whether or not that church is actually changing, this was a light bulb moment for me. At least in the United States, many churches have adopted a model of church based on Hillsong. This model paved the way for smoke machines, contemporary Christian music (eliminating all other forms of worship, such as liturgical, hymnal, gospel, *coritos*, and so on), Christianese subculture, and an emphasis on numbers. Why? Because from the outside, the model looks successful and attractive. But success is not found in numbers, filled seats, or a building.

Success is reaching the lost and edifying the found. Success is churches being known for their justice initiatives. Success is a faith group being known for unity and dignity and not uniformity and disrespect. Success is Christians looking like, sounding like, and being like Jesus—not like each other. Success is a healthy church.

When I was twenty-three, I was lost and had not been to a church in about six years. I had stopped believing in Jesus and the Bible completely, but with the loving support of friends and my boyfriend (now husband), I walked into a church building and it reignited my relationship with Jesus. And you know where that happened? Hillsong New York City. I will never deny all the pain that place caused many people, and I also acknowledge it's where Jesus met me again. Was it the lights? The preaching? The music? No, Jesus was just there because his people were there. And all by myself (not during their version of an altar call), right in my seat, I gave my life to Jesus quietly and privately.

Jesus can use anything anywhere, but what happened after that is that I didn't grow. I didn't know anything about the Bible and living a holy Christian life. I joined a small group and got to know people, but I didn't grow in my biblical understanding there either. Later on, I ended up at a church that I eventually worked at—and didn't grow spiritually there. What I did become an expert in was Christianese (which can make people think someone is spiritually mature when they aren't). I left that spiritually abusive situation and went to another church that somehow I ended up working at, and there too I didn't grow spiritually, mainly because it seemed like the pastor wanted to be the only expert on the Bible. Then 2020 happened, and I spent a few years not being part of a dedicated church community, and you know what happened? I learned about Jesus and the Bible in a real way.

I think every Christian should go to a healthy church and be a part of the edifying and healthy building of the Body. But I had to leave unhealthy places to learn what it means to be a healthy Christian, to be a part of a healthy church, and to grow in a healthy way. I did this not on my own or because of misguided theology. I did this on purpose because I was living as a replica of the Christians surrounding me instead of being like Jesus.

Some call this deconstruction or decolonizing your faith. For me, it was a journey toward truth. Now that I've said the *D* words, I hope you don't run away but consider how those words have been used to divide the church. In fact, most of us have deconstructed at one point or another and should certainly decolonize immediately.

When you gave your life to Jesus, did you stop believing certain things? Did you change some mindsets? Did you unlearn a thing or two? That, my friend, is deconstruction. We've all done it, and it's a healthy thing. Can it be done in an unhealthy way? Absolutely. But that doesn't mean *deconstruction* is a bad word. In fact, it's an invitation to unlearn, relearn, and even repent. Some people end up leaving the faith after going on the journey, some people develop new theologies while on the journey, and some people come to know Jesus in a much truer way after deconstructing. Just because people land in different places while walking this path doesn't make it a bad path.

As a person of color and a woman, I've had to do a heavy amount of both deconstruction and decolonization, because the current Christian culture I am talking about operates in ways that I don't in my everyday life in the Bronx. The current Christian culture leaves no room for the *coritos* (Spanish worship music) I grew up with. The current Christian culture leaves no room for someone who doesn't want to walk into a dark room with flashing lights on a Sunday. The current Christian culture does not welcome me, see me, or consider me in my image-bearing uniqueness. It wants to assimilate me and erase my culture, language, story, ancestry, setting, and traditions. Because none of them fit the Starbucks church model.

The Doctrine of Discovery

Gandhi purportedly said Christians are not like Christ. So we have to consider who we are like. Probably each other because we are determined to create replicas of one another. This is what the mission of colonization was and remains: to go somewhere and make the people, space, and culture just like us. Colonization is quite simple in its mission, and that's why it's been both successful and detrimental. It knows what it wants to do and how to do it.

Have you ever heard of the doctrine of discovery? Let me tell you about it by drawing on Mark Charles and Soong-Chan Rah's book *Unsettling Truths*:

> The doctrine of discovery is a set of legal principles that governed the European colonizing powers, particularly regarding the administration of indigenous land. . . . The doctrine emerged from a series of fifteenth-century papal bulls, which are official decrees by the pope that carry the full weight of his ecclesial office. On June 18, 1452, Pope Nicholas V issued the papal bull *Dum Diversas*, which initiated the first set of documents that would compose the Doctrine of Discovery. The official decree of the pope granted permission to King Alfonso V of Portugal to "invade, search out, capture, vanquish, and subdue all Saracens (Muslims) and pagans whatsoever, and other enemies of Christ wheresoever placed, and all moveable and immovable goods whatsoever held and possessed by them and to *reduce their persons to perpetuate slavery*" (emphasis ours), and to apply and appropriate to himself and his successors the kingdoms, dukedoms, counties, principalities, dominions, possessions, and goods, and to cover them to his and their use and profit.[3]

You did not read that wrong. The pope declared, decreed, and directed this doctrine. This was not an illegal action but a legal one, and in some places in the world, this doctrine is still legal. I recommend you read *Unsettling Truths*.

Let's explore how colonization was perpetuated and elevated by Christians and what that has resulted in today. The purpose of colonization was to invade, capture, and vanquish people who were so-called enemies of Christ. Notice how that language sounds familiar. It sounds like the beginning of John 10:10: "The thief comes only to steal and kill and destroy." The pope decreed that the enemies should be invaded, captured, and vanquished, but Scripture says that the enemy—Satan—is the one who does those things. Capturing sounds a lot like stealing, vanquishing sounds a lot like killing, and invading sounds a lot like destroying. So were these Christians doing the work of Christ or the work of Satan?

John 8:42–44 says:

> Jesus said to them, "If God were your Father, you would love me, for I have come here from God. I have not come on my own; God sent me. Why is my language not clear to you? Because you are unable to hear what I say. You belong to your father, the devil, and you want to carry out your father's desires. He was a murderer from the beginning, not holding to the truth, for there is no truth in him. When he lies, he speaks his native language, for he is a liar and the father of lies."

We don't like to examine this Scripture passage because it could apply to any of us in any given moment. It could mean that we are not living in the truth of Christ or doing his will. But this passage is also a condemnation of the doctrine of discovery, a doctrine of the devil, a doctrine that has allowed the dehumanization, massacre, assault, and diminishment of millions of people in the name of Christ and his mission. This is not the mission and work of Christ. This is not going to the nations and making disciples of them. This is the work of the enemy, one of the foundations and frameworks for colonization.

If we reread the above description of the doctrine of discovery, we'll notice it includes not just people but also things and land. This is what colonization has done throughout history—taken land, people, and culture to erase or dominate them. Often colonizing groups implemented their own ways in the new land. For the Native Americans in the United States, this meant being forced to learn English, put on European apparel, eat things that made them sick, and change their names to something Europeans could pronounce, even though Europeans had no issues pronouncing the names Giovanni Pierluigi da Palestrina, Thoinot Arbeau, and Hieronymus Praetorius (European composers in the 1400s).

In late 2022, Bethel Church, a charismatic California megachurch, announced it would be planting a church in New York City. The announcement included these words: "Many of these cities have become demonic strongholds seeping the cesspool of immorality into society and exporting it around the globe." They were talking about New York City. Again, if you go back to the quote I shared about the doctrine of discovery, you will find a similar tone and message. Later on, the church changed the wording on its website, but it did not publicly repent or apologize for this language used about New York City and its people.

If we look around, we see the doctrine of discovery everywhere. It's in the White church planters who go to a predominantly Black and Latino/a neighborhood to start a church but don't know anyone in the area and don't take the time to learn about the people and the culture of the area. That is colonization displayed.

It's in the worship culture that promotes songs sounding the same and people dressing and sounding the same regardless of worship style, background, or preference. That is colonization ingrained.

It's in walking into a church building anywhere in the country and finding the setup, culture, people, attire, language, and structure being the same as those of many other churches. That is colonization projected.

It's the Starbucks model. It's capitalism. It's consumerism. It's replication. It's whittling away the cultures, histories, and preferences of people so we can all look the same. Not the same as Christ but the same as mainstream, White-led, megachurch Christians whom someone has convinced us we are all supposed to be like.

When Columbus arrived in the new world, he called the people he saw here a name based on what he had seen before in India. He called them Indians, but that's not what they called themselves because that's not what they were. Instead of asking them what they called themselves, he named them. Colonized Christianity doesn't ask—it forces, projects, and creates a culture that becomes such a norm that people submit to it sometimes without realizing that their submission has come at a cost.

Submitting to a church in a Black neighborhood that won't play gospel music.

Submitting to pastors in a Latino neighborhood who won't learn Spanish.

Submitting to a church culture that looks nothing like the city/town the church is in—not in a "let's not be like the world" way but in a "let's forget who's outside the doors" way.

Submitting to being a part of spaces that change who we are.

The church's purpose is not to change culturally, historically, racially, linguistically, or traditionally. It is to edify people so they look like the Christ they are choosing to follow. My culture, gender, ancestry, dialect, history, background, and lifestyle are not sins to be repented of but things to be celebrated and honored in the church I call home and in the Body of Christ that I belong to.

Unity Restores

The word *unity* comes from the Latin word *unitas*, which means "one." I think that's the most powerful aspect of unity; it reminds us that we are *one* Body. We don't have an individualized faith, and the kingdom of God is not ultimately broken down into several separate houses (churches/denominations). If someone has a cold, it mainly lives in the person's head, nose, and throat, but to get better and feel fully restored, that person has to care for their whole body. They need to lie down, sleep, eat healthy food, and care for the different elements of their body so they can recover. This is what unity, if done well in the church, can do. It can restore what has been diseased and sick. It can restore what has been dishonored and disrespected. It can restore what is not healthy. But this is a collective job. It is unity, not uniformity.

Uniformity is the doctrine of discovery, colonization, and the Starbucks model.

Unity is being of one mind while honoring the uniqueness of each image bearer. Unity is working alongside Christ as he helps us move back to the basics of what the church gets to be, what Christian living gets to be, and how people see Christians in the world. Unity is renouncing tribalism, cults, colonization, division, partiality, and celebrity culture.

Unity is choosing to see every person in the Body. So maybe that means we don't use flashing lights at church services and conferences so that our neurodivergent, hearing and visually impaired, and epileptic brothers and sisters don't feel unwelcome or overlooked. According to an online article, "Lighting can create migraines, increase depression symptoms, and decrease our quality of life. For individuals with autism, lighting is even more crucial for their health. Lighting and Autism Spectrum Disorder is a complex issue that is different for each individual."[4] Other sources note that dark rooms can prohibit the hearing impaired from being able to read others' lips, facial expressions, gestures, and sign language.

The use of lights at a worship service started with the "seeker sensitive" movement of the 1990s and 2000s. Bright concert lights were a way to attract younger generations, people who didn't grow up in the church, or people who grew up in the church but left. Hopefully we've realized that being seeker friendly has less to do with visuals and more to do with people and what is taught. People are not impressed by lights; they are looking for the truth. This is just one of many church norms that may seem harmless or not a big deal but should be looked at in a bigger way. If we claim to be a unified Body, then we must make room for everyone. That is unity.

Choosing unity might mean using a community needs assessment instead of assuming we know what a city/neighborhood needs based on biases and outsider perspective. A *community needs assessment* is defined as "a systematic process of identifying the needs or gaps in service of a neighborhood, town, city, or state, as well as the resources and strengths available to meet those needs."[5] This is unity—going into neighborhoods to offer support where it's actually needed, not where we think it's needed.

Choosing unity might mean creating churches and Christian spaces that are committed to amplifying forgotten voices, overlooked communities, and marginalized people—not as a way of pitying, tokenizing, or fulfilling a quota but as a way of acknowledging that these very people have contributed to the Body of Christ locally and effectively for centuries, even if we can't find their stories, testimonies, and work in most Christian history books.

Unity, if done well, could transform how safe people feel in church, how secure they feel in their identity, and how sacred they see the Scriptures.

Unity, if done well, could dismantle the Starbucks church model and restore the church to live out Acts 2:42: "All the believers devoted themselves to the apostles' teaching, and to fellowship, and to sharing in meals (including the Lord's Supper), and to prayer" (NLT).

Unity, if done well, could help people live out Micah 6:8: "He has shown you, O mortal, what is good. And what does the LORD require of you? To act justly and to love mercy and to walk humbly with your God."

This is the way of the radical.

RADICAL THOUGHTS

> Uniformity is being lived out, used, and strategized in more ways than we may realize in the Christian world. It's up to us to open our eyes to notice—with the purpose not to critique it but to change it to unity.

> Unity doesn't mean we agree on all things theologically, but it does mean we agree that Jesus is God and we'll follow him collectively.

> Perhaps a community needs assessment is something you can bring up to your church if it's never been done before.

> Consider whether your church follows the Starbucks church model. Even if your church is a campus or church plant of another church, it shouldn't look the same way as that church because of the difference in location and people.

> Think about the ways you've perhaps submitted to uniformity and how you can return to being yourself.

> If you've planted a church, reflect on how you went through that process and if it was honorable to the people living in the city/town where the church was planted.

REFLECTIVE QUESTIONS

> How have you seen the doctrine of discovery displayed in churches you've been to? Is your church different from that? If not, what can you do to help your church change from uniformity to unity?

> Reflect on the Starbucks church model. Have you gotten so used to how much churches are alike that you would be uncomfortable if they were to change?

> How can you contribute to the unity that God has already established in the Body of Christ?

> In what ways, if any, have you been a part of amplifying uniformity in the Christian world?

RESTORATIVE MEDITATION

INHALE: Jesus, we thank you for making us unique.

EXHALE: Convict us to change so we can repent of uniformity and move toward unity.

INHALE: Lord, we thank you for forming us as one.

EXHALE: Grow our discernment in how we live out that oneness so it is still unique to each member of the Body of Christ.

INHALE: Abba, we ask for your guidance in being like you.

EXHALE: Forgive us for the times we have been like the enemy.

REMAIN IN SCRIPTURE

- Micah 6:8
- John 8:42–44
- John 10:10
- John 17:20–21
- Acts 2:42
- 1 Corinthians 12:12–27

4

Taking Sanctification Seriously

> Christians' most important social task is nothing less than to be a community capable of hearing the story of God we find in the scripture and living in a manner that is faithful to that story.
>
> —Stanley Hauerwas, *A Community of Character*[1]

> Sanctify them by the truth; your word is truth.
>
> —John 17:17

There is deep purpose and profound power in the gift of sanctification. When taken seriously, it can transform the Body of Christ. Much of what is wrong or not working within the Christian world arises from deep and varied roots. One root is that we've forgotten the seriousness of sanctification, or being set apart.

Sanctification is

> the action or process of being freed from sin or purified,
> the action of making or declaring something holy,
> the action of causing something to be or seem morally right or acceptable.[2]

To be sanctified is to be set apart.

I left the church, Jesus, and the faith altogether for about six years, from 2007 to 2013. I believed any philosophy or school of thought except for biblical beliefs during that time. Although there is grief to that season of being so far from God, I'm also grateful for it, because when I did return to Jesus and the church, I had a different eye for things.

I had been in the spoken word scene of New York City for years and had seen greenrooms. The greenrooms weren't any different in Christian spaces. They were a space for specific people and excluded and othered specific people. The same light effects and fog machines I saw at music festivals were used at a Sunday service or Christian conference. The way I saw some people superficially respond to injustice in the world was the way I saw the church do it. The way people were manipulated, abused, hurt, and othered in the world was the way I saw it happen in the church. The way I saw nonprofits I worked for misuse their money was the same way I saw churches I worked for do it. The way I saw people in power abuse that power and not apologize for it in the world was the same way I saw leaders do it within the Body of Christ. And the way I got burned out in the world as a social worker and educator was the same way I got burned out working for a church—the grind and hustle culture were no different.

Now, years later, I notice the differences and see that there are good and faithful churches and Christians. There are Christians who have the Holy Spirit and respond to his convictions and voice. There are churches that don't make a production out of their services. There are Christians who repent publicly if they need to. There are Christian spaces that promote rest and sabbath and don't overwork people. There are communities of Christians that are committed to justice work in a faithful and tangible way.

Christianity is not a complete mess. Christians are not a complete mess. It's important we acknowledge that before we keep going because as you read this book, you may get to a place where you feel and think that is the case. My heart behind this message is that we would be a healthy and whole Body, that we would be sanctuaries, and that other people would believe us to be sanctuaries. But to get to a place where the Body acts like a sanctuary, we have work to do.

Notice how the definition of sanctification above has the word *action* in every line. Sanctification is not a feeling or a thought. It's how we live our lives and how we show up as Christians in the world. To abide in Christ, to walk in obedience to Christ in his radical way—this is the sanctified work we are called to. We are to be so set apart that the differences between us and the world are obvious, not in a self-righteous way but in a way that points people to the one who invites us to sanctification, in a way that shows that the purpose and the power of the cross weren't wasted. This is the way of the radical. That we may be edified, give God glory, and help others see the real

Jesus so they can consider or be curious about the good news he brings.

It would take an entire book to address all the things Christians are called to be sanctified in. Here I address only a few that I think are the most important to making ourselves, our communities, and our churches healthier.

Rest

One of my favorite quotes is from my good friend Ashley Abercrombie. She says, "Rest reminds us that we aren't God."

According to one job search website, 83 percent of people in the United States surveyed deal with work-related stress.

- Forty-four percent of employees experience physical fatigue from work-related stress.
- Seventy-six percent of US workers report that workplace stress affects their personal relationships.
- Depression-induced absenteeism costs US businesses $51 billion a year as well as an additional $26 billion in treatment costs.
- The main causes of workplace stress are workload (39 percent of workers), interpersonal issues (31 percent), juggling work and personal life (19 percent), and job security (6 percent).[3]

These experiences are not far from those found within many churches. I can tell you from firsthand experience. I was a part of a church where leaders kept telling me, "This is not a job; it's a calling." That never sat well with me because, yes, it was a calling, but it was also very much a job. A job I should have had a schedule for and a life outside of, but in that season that wasn't the case. I was overworked, used, manipulated, and burned out, and I was a paid employee (very underpaid in comparison to my pastors/bosses). Volunteers in that church were experiencing many of the same things. The pastors even returned to work one week after having a baby. The staff could have handled things if they had taken a maternity/paternity leave. But they came back to work immediately, communicating the message that rest is not the culture there.

At one staff meeting, we were talking about an event we were going to host on a Saturday. I asked if this meant we'd have Monday off. The room got quiet. There was a long silence until my pastor and boss said I had the wrong heart and should be focused on serving instead of resting. He then continued with the meeting. I spent the rest of the day thinking about that statement and wondering where my heart was and if my question was disrespectful or wrong.

Later that day, I prayed and realized, *Girl, that was not a bad or disrespectful question—it was the right one to ask*. I can't tell you right now if that was my intuition or the Holy Spirit, but I do recall realizing that my thought was valid and biblical. My heart wasn't in the wrong place. It was actually in a very scriptural place. Read what happened after Jesus fed the five thousand, which was more likely fifteen thousand if we include women and children (and we will include them here because women and children are people too): "Immediately Jesus made the disciples get into the boat and go on ahead of him to the other side, while he dismissed the crowd. After he had dismissed them, he went up on a mountainside by himself to pray. Later that night, he was there alone" (Matt. 14:22–23). After serving, Jesus spent time in prayer. He spent time alone. Jesus rested.

What the pastor's comment suggested was that I should pour out without being poured into. I felt manipulated. This kind of narrative has been used to get us to grind and hustle to get to the top, to get more money, and to reach the life of our dreams, but as Christians we know that the life of our dreams is the one God sets before us and calls us to. First Thessalonians 4:11–12 says, "Make it your ambition to lead a quiet life: You should mind your own business and work with your hands, just as we told you, so that your daily life may win the respect of outsiders and so that you will not be dependent on anybody." The apostle Paul communicates to the church in Thessalonica a life that pleases God. In John 10:10, Jesus promises abundant living for all of us. This looks different for everyone, but it certainly should include rest. This is what is right—to listen to Jesus, who promoted, commanded, exemplified, and encouraged rest. Because when we don't take a break from labor, we are telling God . . .

- We don't need you; we can do it ourselves.
- We will strive and hustle because that's what you require of us.
- We will serve until we're burned out.
- We'll be doers unto your name until we can't anymore.

But he graciously responds by saying this is what the church gets to do instead:

It gets to honor the body, mind, heart, and spirit that were once used and now get to rest.

It gets to resist the North American approach to overserving in church.

It gets to honor the humanity in us and the biblical understanding of sabbath.

It gets to restore our dignity as people and not machines.

It gets to reclaim our first calling—which is to be sons and daughters of God.

It gets to renew us and point us toward the truth of what it means to serve others and pour out from a place of fullness and peace.

Plenty of people don't have access to rest because of financial, home, or relational circumstances. Rest is a privilege in our world because we live in a society that has been built and centered on overworking and overusing people.

Because we know this, will the Body of Christ choose to be sanctified in rest?

Will we stop overworking people who serve in our churches?

Will we show up for those who need financial support so they can rest?

Will we teach the value of rest and the importance of sabbath?

Will we be people who are so rested that we can be sacred, soft, and safe toward other believers and the entire world?

These are questions we have to wrestle with. And perhaps we need to repent of some of the answers we have come up with in the past. We do this not out of shame but out of joy that we get to move away from the world's norm and move closer to the rest-filled, sanctified way of the radical one we have chosen to follow.

I'll close this section with a reflection from Cole Arthur Riley in *This Here Flesh*:

> Rest is an act of defiance, and it cannot be predicated on apology. It's the audacity to face the demands of this world and

proclaim, we will not be owned. We will not return to the chains that once held us. They are brittle and tarnished from our tears, which made the flood. Remember. You were never meant to prove your dignity. You, whose flesh contains more bodies than your own. You don't belong in the catacombs of restlessness, wandering from death to life. Lie down with me in the pasture, where life is alive and growing with the unapologetic slowness of a blade of grass.[4]

Dignity

Dignity is connected to rest because our lack of resting and our overworking of other people within the church are very much a dignity problem. According to *Merriam-Webster*, *dignity* means "the state or quality of being worthy, honored, or esteemed."[5]

There are two extremes concerning the word *worthy* within the Christian world. On one side are people who highlight that God said humans are good, so this means we deserve good things and are worthy of every good thing headed our way. Then there are those who say we are worthless. We are fundamentally sinners who deserve hell, and that's it. Neither side captures the witness of Scripture. More than any other place, the cross is where we find our human worthiness. The cross is what communicates our worth. Every human being has dignity because, first, we are made in the image of God, and second, God loved us enough to save us. If we weren't worthy of anything, then he wouldn't have sent Jesus, and if we were deserving of all good things, then we wouldn't need the cross. The cross restored the original "goodness" he formed us with, and with that come honor and respect.

Our world disregards human dignity in many ways—even in ways we don't consider or think about. When we think about the US prison system or how food is processed or how injustices are handled, we can clearly see a lack of dignity. We see a lack of dignity in the pornography industry and in magazines solely focused on gossiping about people's lives. From macro to micro, the world is not an expert in dignity. But Christ is.

We must see dignity in all people, but we must first address a lack of dignity with fellow brothers and sisters in Christ. As we'll explore in parts 2 and 3 of this book, we are missing the mark in many ways in relation to how Christians feel dignified by others. Every church abuse experience involves a lack of dignity. Every scandal or documentary that comes out shows leaders and institutions showing a lack of dignity. Every comment disrespecting another believer for thinking something different from us is a missed opportunity to dignify someone else.

We have work to do in the area of dignity, and it starts with understanding that there is worthiness in every human being because of what Christ did and still does. Jesus went to the cross for every one of us.

So how can we be sanctified in this area? We can honor people's opinions. We can treat them with dignity even if we don't affirm everything they believe or think. Someone recently reached out to me to share they really like what I'm about and how I talk so much about dignity and justice. They asked about my view on LGBTQIA+ inclusion. I responded by saying I believe people in the LGBTQIA+ community are image bearers worthy of dignity and love and also that I hold to the biblical and historical Christian sexual ethic. This person responded by calling me homophobic and demon possessed, without knowing me, my life, my decisions, or my thoughts. I responded to the person with dignity and they dismissed me anyway.

What I think and believe should not determine how I'm treated, even if people disagree with me. Because of Christ and the cross, I deserve dignity. The same is true for others. I did not attack this person because they are an image bearer worthy of dignity. And they may have experienced deep trauma around their sexuality—especially within the church. They may have experienced Christians being homophobic and dehumanizing toward them. I love them regardless (even though I don't know them personally), and I chose to respond to them with dignity, even after they said I'm demon possessed and even though I don't align with what they think and believe, because they are a beloved image bearer of God worthy of honor.

I'm a Black Latina woman who is a daughter of immigrants; some people disagree with the very fact that I am breathing, living, working, or even writing this book. And every single one of those people is still an image bearer whom God loves and I love. The truth is we won't change most people's minds, but that doesn't mean we get to disrespect or dishonor them. Sanctification is needed to uphold dignity.

Celebrity Culture

I'm not one to love a greenroom. At the annual conference I host, Sowers Summit, speakers and volunteers alike are in the same space, sharing meals together and connecting. Now, as someone who does public speaking, I understand that speakers may need a moment of privacy before the conference, which is why we have space for that as well. But the greenroom is for all volunteers, teams, and speakers. I remember I shared a post about this on Instagram, and I received several responses from people saying that we need to give "giants" in the faith privacy because some people don't know how to act around them. This is an example of why we are talking about celebrity culture and sanctification. How did we get to a place where the church has a celebrity culture like the world does, and so much so that we feel we need to give those people a special place? It breaks my heart.

Some Christians strive to become celebrities by saying out-of-the-box, unbiblical, or dishonorable things. And then there are people who have come to be well-known based on healthy ministry or stewarding their gifts. It's important we don't put all those people in the same category. I like to distinguish between celebrities and those who have become known for their faithful works. But that's a difference in approach and integrity, not humanity. Both types of people fall short like the rest of us, so if we fear that volunteers or other people will ask for an autograph or not leave them alone, then we must address this problem in our churches. We should preach and teach more on partiality, gifts, and seeing all image bearers the same.

Famous people don't become famous by themselves. I know you can buy Instagram followers these days, but most famous people become famous because actual people, not bots, elevate them. We buy their books, we go to their churches and conferences, we listen to their podcasts, we watch their YouTube channels, we follow them on Instagram, and we buy everything they sell. I'm not saying we shouldn't support certain people, but we should consider the *why* behind our support. Do we want to listen to them or learn from them because they are a celebrity Christian or because they have biblical knowledge to teach?

This again highlights that every challenge and concern within the Body of Christ is a collective issue. This is not one person's problem—it's ours. We get to contribute to the health of the Body by acknowledging that we admire some people and that it is okay to do so but that once we've put them in a place of celebrity, we have made them idols. Just read the Old Testament and you'll see over and over what happens when people make and worship idols instead of God.

There is partiality in the world, but there can't be in the kingdom of God due to gifting, position, or being known. We must be set apart from the world in all ways, including this one. If the world has influencers, we should instead have people making an impact. If the world has celebrities, we should instead have Christ-centered teachers discipling us. If the world has systems and structures of partiality, we should instead create a culture where pews, platforms, and pulpits don't determine your worth. A consecrated sanctuary.

Accountability

According to the Pew Research Center, the term *cancel culture* comes from a 1980s song in which the word *cancel* means breaking up with someone. Pew notes that "over the past several years, cancel culture has become a deeply contested idea in the nation's political discourse. There are plenty of debates over what it is and what it means, including whether it's a way to hold people accountable, or a tactic to punish others unjustly, or a mix of both."[6]

When a person is "canceled" in media and politics, it often just means they disappear for a while and then eventually come back or they share an apology post on their social media to come back even quicker. Is the Body of Christ set apart from the world in this area? Are leaders who lack moral integrity able to come back to the spotlight without true repentance? Many public figures in the church seem to come back, apologize (sometimes), and continue to work, be famous, and make money.

So how can we as the Body choose to be different in this?

In John 8, a woman caught in adultery is about to be stoned—or canceled—and Jesus steps in with both grace and truth and confronts the Pharisees, because they weren't being graceful and truthful. When they leave, Jesus says this to the woman:

> "Woman, where are they? Has no one condemned you?"
>
> "No one, sir," she said.
>
> "Then neither do I condemn you," Jesus declared. "Go now and leave your life of sin." (vv. 10–11 CSB)

We don't talk enough about these words of Jesus. We can misunderstand and assume he just let her go, but he tells her not to sin anymore. What does this mean? If I have a sin problem and want to stop, and I feel like God is telling me to stop, I can't just magically stop. I need a community to hold me accountable. I need some sort of recovery or learning process depending on the kind of sin it is. I need to be in the Word of God to learn more about how God feels about this sin. Jesus doesn't tell her, "Go and grow." He tells her, "Go and repent and be free of this." He tells her to go and do something about it.

Jesus is graceful and truthful. He tells her to go and sin no more, but she knows this doesn't mean just saying sorry and continuing her life as if nothing happened. In her case, she didn't sin in a way that affected many if any other people, whereas often the people we want to cancel have harmed others or done something deeply un-Christlike. Our desire to cancel comes from a place of wanting to see justice and truth lived out, but even then we must repent of wanting to see people canceled. Instead, we should want to see redemption for all people, no matter what they've done. That is the way of the radical.

Accountability is different from cancel culture. It's the sanctified approach to addressing someone who has sinned, especially if they have sinned against someone else. Every case where a Christian sins against someone requires accountability, whether publicly or privately. The sanctified way of the radical includes accountability. Sometimes this means stepping down from a position at a church or taking time to go to a recovery place to heal and get better. However it looks, it involves more than an apology. Apologies matter, but the actions that follow matter more.

Repentance

The world has apologies and remorse; Christians have repentance. This is one of the most powerful and loving tools God has given humanity. It's something that sets us free, edifies us, and glorifies God.

In 2023, Rick Warren publicly repented for his long-held views on women preaching and pastoring. Warren belongs to a denomination that doesn't allow women to be pastors or to preach on Sundays or anywhere where both men and women are present, and he supported this theology for decades. But in 2023, he changed his mind and publicly repented. He didn't just repent; he also went to the denomination he belonged to and asked leaders to reconsider the role of women in the church. The leaders did not agree to change their theology or their minds, but he remained firm in his newfound knowledge.

I don't personally know Rick Warren, so I don't know his motives or his story of how he got here, but that was a bold move because he risked not just a few people disagreeing with him but millions, and yet his conviction trumped that. He was willing to be sanctified even if it meant millions would disagree with him, cancel him, or not support him.

Repentance is a scary word for some of us. The first time I heard repentance being taught in a biblical way was back in 2017 on social media by my friend Jess Connolly. I remember her talking about it a few times and thinking, How is she talking about this so casually? I was in shock by how transparent she talked about it, because I had always connected that word with shame and condemnation based on what I had been taught growing up. But then one day I came across Romans 2:4: "Or do you show contempt for the riches of his kindness, forbearance and patience, not realizing that God's kindness is intended to lead you to repentance?"

I couldn't believe my eyes. God's kindness and my repentance are connected? One of the ways we walk in the way of the radical and are sanctified is by talking more about topics that are important to Jesus. He literally began his ministry talking about repentance: "From that time on Jesus began to preach, 'Repent, for the kingdom of heaven has come near'" (Matt. 4:17).

The world struggles to apologize, forgive, reconcile, and change minds. As the Body of Christ, we get to be sanctified and live a different way, even if it comes with a sacrifice.

So how do we respond to the call to sanctification? By choosing to be healthy, humble, and holy. Healthy Christians live in God's Word and apply it to all life's circumstances. Humble Christians see the world and others as God does and live in deep awareness of their own sin. Holy Christians choose to honor and glorify God in every setting and situation of life. This isn't easy, but it's also not something we are meant to figure out or live out on our own. The Spirit of the living God is within you. Rely on him.

RADICAL THOUGHTS

> Rest is not earned and indeed is productive.
> Opportunities to dignify people are presented to us several dozen times a day, and it's our responsibility to respond to the invitations in a sanctified way.
> Celebrities are made by people. If that is true, then that means Christians have created Christian celebrities and we are also the ones who can change that.
> Churches should have accountability structures that are transparent and biblical.
> Repentance is a practice, discipline, and gift that gets to be a part of the regular rhythms of our lives.

REFLECTIVE QUESTIONS

> How can you grow in being healthy?
> How can you grow in being humble?
> How can you grow in being holy?
> How can you grow in being helpful?

RESTORATIVE MEDITATION

INHALE: Lord, guide me toward being set apart as a healthy, humble, holy member of the Body,

EXHALE: so I can be a helpful representative of your kingdom here on earth.

REMAIN IN SCRIPTURE

- o Matthew 4:17
- o Matthew 14:22–23
- o John 8:10–11
- o John 10:10
- o John 17:17
- o Romans 2:4
- o 1 Thessalonians 4:11–12

The Body I Now See

The Body I now see holds the stories of people with care and with no forgetfulness that every part of the Body lives in the likeness of Elohim.

The Body I now see communes and communicates in a way that creates ripples of miracles on earth and rejoicing melodies in heaven.

The Body I now see takes the veil being torn off seriously by knowing that our freedom is tied to one another.

The Body I now see celebrates a tapestry of colors, sizes, sounds, perspectives, and experiences so as to acknowledge the beauty within each created being made by God.

The Body I now see holds the living, inked words found in the Word of God as the only way, truth, and life.

The Body I now see is one that is unified in a way that makes hell tremble and the holy One be glorified.

The Body I now see is one that I am a part of, and I will commit to restoring her broken pieces all the days of my life.

The Body I now see is the Body of Christ—healthy, whole, humble, hopeful, and holy, as the Potter intended.

PART 2

Soft—From Collision to Compassion

If we have no peace, it is because we have forgotten that we belong to each other.

—Mother Teresa

5

A Call to Collective Suffering, or Practicing Presence

> When it's all said and done, I don't care to be remembered as a powerhouse. I hope to be remembered as a safe home.
>
> —Tori Hope Petersen[1]

> For we do not have a high priest who is unable to empathize with our weaknesses, but we have one who has been tempted in every way, just as we are—yet he did not sin.
>
> —Hebrews 4:15 ESV

The two titles of this chapter are meant to convey what trauma-informed living looks like. Trauma-informed support is finding many alternatives, options, and words to comfort and support people in their suffering. It's not deciding there is one way to heal, grieve, suffer, or keep going. Trauma is one of the buzziest words out there these days, so it's helpful to know the definition. Here is one definition from trauma expert Bessel Van Der Kolk, author of the bestselling book *The Body Keeps the Score*: "Trauma is much more than a story about the past that explains why people are frightened, angry or out of control. Trauma is re-experienced in the present, not as a story, but as profoundly disturbing physical sensations and emotions that may not be consciously associated with memories of past trauma."[2]

Trauma is what our hearts and minds experience as a result of being in a painful, shocking, or challenging situation, experience, or circumstance—often (but not always) out of our control. People can have different responses to the very same traumatic experience. Therefore, being trauma informed means seeking to understand the impact a trauma has had on someone and aiming to help them recover by being mindful of how we talk to, care for, resource, and support that person. This is in the way of Jesus, who responds to our pain, past, and problems with compassion and a very specific, unique approach to our stories, feelings, and minds.

I lost my dad in a plane accident when I was eleven years old. Over two hundred other people on that plane also passed away, and I'm sure some of them had children as well. Jesus did not meet me and the children of the other victims in the same way, because we probably didn't react or respond to the trauma in the same way. He met us where we were and with what we needed in that moment for comfort, peace, and our own mourning. For example, my fifteen- and nineteen-year-old brothers also lost their dad that day, and in the years to come,

Jesus met my brothers differently based on what they needed and how the trauma affected them. Jesus doesn't change, but he does approach people according to their unique stories and sadness. We see this repeatedly in the Bible, and this is precisely what the church gets to do.

The purpose of this section of the book is to examine the radical way of being soft with one another. Another way of saying this is being trauma-informed people. We move past colliding with one another because of differences and draw closer to one another through compassion. We exhibit the Spirit-produced fruit of kindness and gentleness—regardless of our gender, experience, culture, background, and life. Gentleness is not just for some people but a fruit that can be produced within all of us and expressed through all of us, according to Galatians 5:22–23. Because, after all, since we are the Body, we have the Holy Spirit.

Discomfort with Presence

If we are going to talk about being soft, or trauma informed, we first must discuss why we don't meet people in their suffering well. The answer is simple: we are uncomfortable with grief and suffering. We feel hopeless because sometimes we can't do anything to change the circumstance. We feel awkward not knowing the right words to say. We feel uncomfortable because someone is crying and we aren't sure how to comfort them. We perhaps are triggered because of their pain and suffering, and so we distance ourselves. We don't know what to do in silence, so we fill the void with savior complex comments like "Everything happens for a reason" that aren't helpful in those moments (or really ever).

Being trauma informed means we don't just spew out things like "I consider that our present sufferings are not worth comparing with the glory that will be revealed in us" (Rom. 8:18). Just because Scripture is true doesn't mean it's always timely or meant to be communicated at every moment—not even Jesus did that. Another passage that tends to be thrown out when someone is suffering is Romans 5:3–4: "Not only so, but we also glory in our sufferings, because we know that suffering produces perseverance; perseverance, character; and character, hope." I graciously invite you to keep Romans out of your mouth when trying to comfort people in grief and suffering. Just kidding, but not really.

In all of this, we realize that we are deeply in need of wisdom. We are looking for answers within ourselves that the Bible and God already have. James 1:5 says, "If any of you lacks wisdom, you should ask God, who gives generously to all without finding fault, and it will be given to you." We need to ask God for wisdom so we can practice presence well with others.

What else do we need to be trauma informed?

We need empathy.
We need awareness.
We need to be prayerful.
We need to be willing to be uncomfortable.
And we need to admit that we are uncomfortable with grief and suffering.

What if the remedy is that we enter the discomfort anyway? We grow and mature. We overcome the awkwardness and embrace the silence. Trauma entails going through something that we likely had no control over. Trauma-informed living or care is considering the trauma of others when talking with, interacting with, or supporting them. The words we speak include options, invitations, and considerations instead of direct advice, next steps, and hurried solutions. The Body of Christ is not Christ. We don't need to try to save. We just need to be soft.

Sometimes, without meaning to, we retraumatize someone or push them toward solitude with the things we say. Now, some may think, Well, nothing's safe to say these days because everyone gets offended and I have to be politically correct. Although there's some truth here, if that is where our thinking lies when trying to navigate how to be soft for others, then we'll simply end up not showing up for them at all. And that's one more person the enemy gets to grab ahold of in their pain and suffering to lead them toward hopelessness.

In our suffering, we can lose sight of God and God's goodness. In our isolation and loneliness, we can find all the reasons not to believe God, his Word, or even his people. This is why grief and suffering should be collective.

First Corinthians 12:26 says, "If one part suffers, every part suffers with it; if one part is honored, every part rejoices with it." Paul is talking to the church in Corinth about unity and diversity within the Body of Christ, and one of his closing remarks is this verse. He says that everything should be done unified, both the rejoicing and the suffering. We are really good at rejoicing together, and I believe we can also get really good at suffering together.

Jesus's Trauma-Informed Way

In Matthew 9:18–19, we see one of the many examples of Jesus's trauma-informed approach to people. Someone says to Jesus,

"'My daughter has just died. But come and put your hand on her, and she will live.' Jesus got up and went with him, and so did his disciples." Jesus responds by going to where the person needs him to be and supporting the person there. By contrast, many churches tell people to come to Sunday service or a prayer service to get healed, be in community, and get support. They say, "Come as you are," but Jesus does something different. He goes to where they are (more on this in chap. 10).

Matthew 9:20–22 continues with a story many of us know, the story of the woman with the issue of blood: "Just then a woman who had been subject to bleeding for twelve years came up behind him and touched the edge of his cloak. She said to herself, 'If I only touch his cloak, I will be healed.' Jesus turned and saw her. 'Take heart, daughter,' he said, 'your faith has healed you.' And the woman was healed at that moment."

Now, we may not be able to multitask like Jesus did, so if you have the capacity to serve only one person at a time in their suffering, I feel you. Do that with no shame. But we can't miss something important that Jesus does here. The language he uses is trauma informed. As the literal Savior of the universe, he doesn't ask what she's done to try to get better or to stop her suffering. Jesus acknowledges that her action shows she wants to be healed, and he meets her there with kind, loving, and welcoming words. He doesn't consider her a distraction, although his disciples probably thought she was. He meets the woman in her suffering, and he provides her with healing. He provides what she needs based on what she expresses she needs. In this case, she doesn't need to use words because Jesus is God.

Matthew 9:23–26 continues: "When Jesus entered the synagogue leader's house and saw the noisy crowd and people playing pipes, he said, 'Go away. The girl is not dead but asleep.' But they laughed at him. After the crowd had been put outside, he went in and took the girl by the hand, and she got up. News of this spread through all that region."

I'm not going to act like I didn't chuckle when I read that Jesus told the flute players to leave. If you need some context, in those times, people were hired to be mourners so no one would have to mourn alone (which is kind of the whole point of this chapter and a beautiful tradition to have). But Jesus's trauma-informed approach is one we can't miss and should learn from. He communicates that we should support people by helping them live in the present reality and not presume the worst or go down a rabbit hole of what-ifs with them—which is what many people do during grief and suffering. He tells the people they are mistaken, that she isn't dead but asleep. He helps the people be present in their bodies, minds, and hearts without rushing toward the possibilities (especially painful or negative ones) the future may hold. Now, let's be clear. He is saying this from a place of knowing, and that's important to see here because trauma messes with our minds, memories, and emotions. Being the Body means we help people come back to reality, graciously and not forcefully, so that they heal and grieve in a healthy state of mind.

Later, Matthew 9:36–38 says, "When he saw the crowds, he had compassion on them, because they were harassed and helpless, like sheep without a shepherd. Then he said to his disciples, 'The harvest is plentiful but the workers are few. Ask the Lord of the harvest, therefore, to send out workers into his harvest field.'" Jesus sees that the crowds are going through many hard things, and he knows they need pastoring, support, leadership, discipleship, and community. He says there is a lot of work to do and not many around to do it. Those who are around need to take the work seriously and shepherd the people who are depressed and dejected. Often verses 37 and 38 are used for church-planting encouragement and to get people to serve, but we can't miss the context of verse 36. In verse 36, Jesus communicates that the workers need to be shepherds—especially for those who need love, support, prayer, compassion, resources, and the good news.

What a responsive and kind God we serve. He sees the suffering and offers solutions and approaches that will serve his people well because he knows his people. And this God came to earth in human form as a man. This is an important thing not to overlook, especially as we talk about being soft, trauma informed, and gentle. Philippians 2:7 says that he "made himself nothing by taking the very nature of a servant, being made in human likeness." Although Jesus was fully God, he was also fully a human being and lived in the male gender.

In my Dominican culture, there is a high expectation for men to be a certain way in their behavior, attire, communication, and mindset. Some would call it toxic masculinity, but I consider it machismo that was planted through colonization and has evolved in unhealthy ways that are now a norm and expectation. God most definitely formed us on purpose in our cultures, races, and ethnicities, but we must remember that we are followers of Jesus before anything else. So even if the culture we live in, the race we are a part of, or the ethnicity we come from holds certain expectations of what it means to "be a man" (or a woman), we must remember that we are sanctuaries. This means we live a life that reflects and glorifies Jesus, not a life that our culture or society expects of us because of our gender, race, age, relationship status, or anything else that is connected to labels or identity. Because this is true, both men and women get to be like Jesus in communication, behavior, and mindset. We can all be gentle, kind, loving, graceful, peaceful, merciful, and trauma informed, regardless of our gender or the expectations society has placed on our gender.

Suffer Prayerfully with All, and Suffer Intimately with Your People

When we hear horrible news, whether through the media or from a friend's friend, we get to pray for people and do whatever we can for them. We suffer with them from a distance by praying (or taking some sort of justice step). But then there's intimate suffering. We suffer intimately with those God has called us to or placed in our lives. We show up for them.

As I mentioned earlier, my dad passed away in a plane that was headed to the Dominican Republic, which is where we are from. The plane was in the sky for only a few seconds before it went right back down, killing all the people onboard and some people on the ground too. I was in the seventh grade when all of this happened, and it was also two months after 9/11, so we were all a bit rattled already, especially since we live in New York City.

Much of my life in that moment and season is a blur, but do you want to know what isn't? The church. West End Presbyterian Church was the community we were a part of at that time and that had been my home church since I was five years old. For the first few weeks and months after we lost my dad, people from our church were consistently at our home, feeding us, caring for us, praying for us, and making sure we were all well. This was done differently for each of us—myself, my mom, and my brothers. We all had different needs, and the church served them all. People created schedules and took shifts. They invited people in our building to support us as well, and our neighbors started showing up. They connected with my school, and I began to meet with a grief counselor twice a week at school. They made sure someone dropped me off and picked me up from school each day.

The church chose to suffer intimately with us by sacrificing their time, money, and energy, by being present with us in our grief and suffering.

Sometimes we forget what it means to suffer with others because we are constantly inviting them out or to come to us (like in a Sunday service). But if we go to where they are, we would realize that their dishes have been dirty for three days because they haven't had the headspace to do that task. We'd see that their fridge is almost empty and they've been eating crackers with peanut butter for a week because they don't have the energy (or maybe the funds) to buy groceries or cook. We'd realize that they are "on" at work and spend seven to nine hours a day suppressing their feelings while crying on their lunch break. We'd see the real story behind their emotion stuffing and grief. And not just the story but how the story is breaking their entire life. We don't all grieve well. We haven't all been given the tools to do it. We shouldn't be judged for that. Rather, we should be met with compassion regardless of how we grieve. And if someone "grieves well," that doesn't mean we check on them any less often.

This is all to say that we get to *really* follow Jesus when it comes to suffering. He modeled it best, and we have his perfect example of how to be soft, to be tender and gentle with those who are suffering and grieving. He was being the church to people long before he asked us to be one.

This is what it is to be a trauma-informed Body of Christ. This is what it looks like to take God's Word seriously and apply it to the practicalities of everyday life. Because the truth for the foreseeable future is that suffering will continue. Therefore, we get to be the church that meets the suffering where they are. That provides those who are suffering with what they need most in their time of grief. That responds to them like Jesus does. We get to move in the way of the radical, which is to practice presence.

Many Scripture passages tell us that God is with us. He was with Adam and Eve in the garden. He chose to come down to be with us as Jesus. And he is still with us right now as the received gift of the Holy Spirit. He has been practicing presence since the beginning of time. If we want to be more like Christ, then we too must practice presence with others.

In the next few chapters, we'll look at how to be soft with those who have been wounded by the church, the marginalized, and the silenced. To suffer well collectively, we need to understand each other. That's what empathy is—understanding someone even if we don't share their suffering or lived experience. We miss the mark when we think we need to have experienced what someone else did to have compassion for them. That's a lie the enemy of our souls wants us to believe to keep us divided.

We fight division in the Spirit by showing up for others in their suffering.

RADICAL THOUGHTS

> You are no one's savior, and you're not expected to be.

> Your presence is a good enough gift.

> Embrace silence as a space for the Holy Spirit to minister to the person you're with.

> Being soft is not a female trait but an image bearer trait. Jesus is soft, and we are his image bearers. Therefore, we can all be soft.

REFLECTIVE QUESTIONS

> What memories can you recall when you experienced people being trauma informed / soft with you? What made those experiences trauma informed?

> What memories can you recall when you didn't experience someone being trauma informed / soft with you? What made those experiences not feel trauma informed?

> How have you seen Jesus be trauma informed with you?

> Are there instances you need to repent of when you harmed someone while thinking you were helping them?

> What is one practical, new thing you can begin to do for people in your life who are suffering?

RESTORATIVE MEDITATION

INHALE: I don't need to carry the suffering of the whole world.
EXHALE: God alone is enough to care for all people.

INHALE: I am committed to practicing presence with those suffering around me.
EXHALE: I am committed to being prayerful for the suffering of the world.

INHALE: I am grateful for how Jesus has met me in my suffering.
EXHALE: I am honored to be a comfort for those who need comforting.

REMAIN IN SCRIPTURE

- o Matthew 9:18–26
- o Matthew 9:36–38
- o 1 Corinthians 12:26
- o Galatians 5:22–23
- o Hebrews 4:15
- o James 1:5

6

A Place for the Weary, Wounded, and Wandering

You're not wrong to hurt / you're not wrong for wanting more / He has always been what you're looking for.

—"You're Not Wrong" by Common Hymnal[1]

> Praise be to the God and Father of our Lord Jesus Christ, the Father of compassion and the God of all comfort, who comforts us in all our troubles, so that we can comfort those in any trouble with the comfort we ourselves receive from God. For just as we share abundantly in the sufferings of Christ, so also our comfort abounds through Christ.
>
> —2 Corinthians 1:3–5

Part of being a soft person and a soft Body of Christ is knowing who needs deep levels of that tenderness and who has been forgotten. We can go all over the world and do missions work and tell people of the gospel in our neighborhoods, while the people in our houses of worship are being abused, are discouraged by modern Christianity, or are confused by what the faith entails. That's who the weary, wounded, and wandering are. They are the people being judged, abandoned, and overlooked by many in the church. If we want to be a healthy Body and glorify God, then we must pay attention to them. Because they matter, because they are members of the Body, and because they need us just as much as we need them.

The Weary

The weary are those who are deeply exhausted by the state of the church. They are over the smoke machines and excessive lights. They can't bear to read one more article about scandal or see another social media or news outlet "apology" by a leader who "fell" into sin. They are confused about how and why Christians are acting the way they are. They can't seem to understand why so many churches are focused on leadership development instead of discipleship. They have been struggling to find a healthy church for a while now. They are hurt by the number of other people who have been hurt by the church and by seeing those very churches and communities not changing. They love God's Word and are distressed by how people use their different interpretations to dehumanize, disrespect, and dishonor others. They are disgusted at how Christian nationalism (which is the idea that the United States is a Christian nation and that the government should adhere to Christian beliefs—that's a very short definition; to learn more, read *American Idolatry* by Andrew L. Whitehead) has found a home in the church and how people don't see what's wrong with this.

People are weary. Maybe you are one of the weary people, or maybe you're a leader of the weary people. Maybe you are friends with this group of people or find yourself moving in the direction of being one of them. If you are someone who is weary, I'm sorry. I apologize for how the church is making you weary. I get it. I've been where you are, and in some ways, I am still where you are. Being weary is different from being hurt because we don't need healing. What we need is renewed hope. We need to fight against all the ways the enemy wants us to leave the faith, the church, and Jesus because of this weariness. We need to fight against being so weary that we become passive Christians who show no signs of spiritual vitality. It's truly a battle.

Many verses can encourage us when we are weary, but my favorite is Isaiah 40:28: "Do you not know? Have you not heard? The LORD is the everlasting God, the Creator of the ends of the earth. He will not grow tired or weary, and his understanding no one can fathom." The reason this is my favorite is because it proclaims the truth of God's unchanging character. Even when we are weary, he is not. When we are tired, he is not.

In trauma-informed support, we get to be what people can't be in that moment. Although there is comfort in someone feeling the same way we do when we are going through something so we don't feel alone, there's also a deep power in being in a space with someone who can carry what we can't.

If we can't carry hope, we need people around us who are hopeful.

If we can't carry joy, we need people around us who are joyful.

If we can't carry peace, we need people around us who have peace.

The Isaiah passage shows us that God will not grow weary even when we do. What a trauma-informed God! He will not grow faint when we do. He is full when we have a limit to our capacity. He is exactly what we need in every moment of our lives. We can't always be this for all people in every circumstance, but if we can help one person at a time, that is good enough.

Those who are weary of the church need hope. Their hope will mainly come from seeing evidence that what they have seen is not the whole picture. They need to see that not all pastors are abusive. They need to see that not all churches are fluffy or superficial. They need to see Christians caring about justice and dignity. They need to witness these things alongside the work the Holy Spirit is already doing within them to grow their hope for a renewal to happen within them.

Sometimes helping the weary looks like listening to them instead of debating something they communicated about the church that discourages them. It can look like having conversations with them that are healthy about a topic we don't agree on. It can look like living life with them instead of just seeing them on Sundays for a service. It can look like inviting them to healthy Christian spaces and communities we belong to or know of.

Helping the weary puts us in the ring with the Lord. Too often we pray for the weary and hope God will renew their hearts and minds without doing our part to contribute to their hope growth. But Jesus invites us to be the church, to be a place for the weary to land softly and feel safe.

The Wounded

The wounded are those who have been hurt, harmed, abused, or traumatized by the church. I like to use "wounded" to mean all those things instead of "hurt" because sometimes "hurt" can feel minimizing to people and because wounds look different for everyone. Some wounds are deep cuts, while others are surface cuts that heal quicker. Some wounds are internal, while others are external. Some wounds affect our whole life, while others affect only one area.

I believe the word *hurt* has become popular because it doesn't affect us as much as *wounded* does. If I stub my toe on the dresser, I'll say it hurts a little. I wouldn't use the word *harm*, *wound*, *trauma*, or *abuse*. But what the wounded are going through is severe because they are an image bearer being dehumanized, undignified, manipulated, or abused by another fellow image bearer. This is harmful, and if we begin to use the words *abused*, *traumatized*, *wounded*, and *harmed*, I think people will respond to these situations differently and more urgently.

The first thing to know about the wounded is that they aren't a monolith; their stories and wounds vary. I went through spiritual abuse in the first church I worked for. At the second church I worked for, I experienced vicarious trauma, manipulation, and being used. My experiences are not the same as those of someone who was sexually abused by someone within the Body of Christ or someone whose money was stolen by the church. There are countless examples of church wounds that have not been my experience. So we must never put all wounded people in the same box. And we must never treat them or approach them the same way.

The second thing to know about the wounded is that on top of being wounded, they are probably also weary, and that's a heavy mix to live with. They are trying to heal while also trying to keep a healthy picture of the church. Sometimes doing both feels impossible. It's a perfect time for the Body of Christ to step in with a radical sense of softness and love. To help them feel seen, heard, and known. To maybe even repent. Beth Allison Barr says, "It seems to me that—instead of spending so much time targeting the faith deconstruction movement as dangerous, vilifying those who have been harmed and walked away—we should be begging forgiveness for how we let corruption rot us from the inside and harm so many people in the name of Jesus."[2]

The Wandering

When it comes to wandering, I think of two groups of people. One is made up of those we are called to evangelize, those who are lost in terms of not knowing Jesus or calling him Savior. The other wandering group is made up of those who are found but are moving away from what they've known Christianity to be throughout their lives. Some would call this deconstruction. Both are wandering and both are looking for answers, and as the church we get to love both.

Let's first talk about the lost group. Matthew 28:19–20 says, "Therefore go and make disciples of all nations, baptizing them in the name of the Father and of the Son and of the Holy Spirit, and teaching them to obey everything I have commanded you." These verses are for not just pastors, priests, or prophets but every person who claims that Jesus is Lord and Savior. That's you and me, my friend. We get so caught up in inviting friends to church so they can hear a good word from the preacher and come to know Jesus that we forget they can come to know Jesus by witnessing us in our living room or while we're taking a walk one day. We overcomplicate the invitation to salvation by thinking it can happen only on a Sunday by someone on a stage asking people to pray the sinner's prayer. But then what happens? Does the person get discipled? Does the person know how to study the Bible? Does the person know what to do when the temptation of sin comes up for them? I'm not saying churches shouldn't have altar calls or an invitation to salvation. They absolutely should, but we have misunderstood our role in this.

We are the church—the everyday saints trying to spread the light of Christ and live in integrity. And because we are, we can invite people to a life with Jesus and then afterward be the very people who disciple them, give them Bible study resources, or do a Bible study with them. We can be the people they call when they are struggling with sin or temptation, and we can be the people who gently walk them toward repentance. We can be the very Body Jesus calls us to be in Matthew 28. And it's not just that we *can* do these things. We absolutely should. We need to be the healthy place and people wanderers have been seeking.

When I left the church, the faith, and Jesus at age seventeen, I was starting college and decided that none of that Christian stuff was real. For five years I searched and searched. I wandered and then came back to Jesus. When I gave my life to Jesus again at a Sunday service, it was not during an altar call but during a very "nonspiritual" moment during the service of a megachurch in New York City. And what happened afterward? I kept having sex with my boyfriend, I still sometimes smoked marijuana, and I kept lying. So much of my heart, mind, and life changed, but so much stayed the same. Jesus changed my life, but I also needed Jesus people around me to help me become consistent in that change. But there was no one to do that. Even the friends who invited me to that Sunday service weren't equipped to do that. Because this is what churches often do. They train people to be "bringers" but not "the Body." They tell people to bring wanderers to services so they can know Jesus instead of encouraging people to show the wandering what Jesus is like through their own lives. The wandering aren't looking for a shiny Jesus with an encouraging word on a stage. The wandering, like all of us, are looking for the truth. We know the truth—it is a person—and so our role is to show him by being the Body.

Then there are the wandering souls who are deconstructing. This is also not a monolithic group. It includes people who have left legalistic churches, abusive communities, and bad theologies. Some of these people are struggling and moving toward no Christian faith at all, while some are walking toward a deeper understanding of Christ on the deconstruction journey. What all these people have in common is that they are trying to unlearn the false gospel that's been taught to them. They are trying to learn who the true God is. So much of this learning has to do with how the Body shows up for them.

So how can we be a trauma-informed people and place for these wanderers? By being soft. Too many are ready to call those who are deconstructing heretics and heathens, but really many of them are just looking for help to find the real Jesus. They understandably are struggling to find him in mainstream modern Christianity. So we get to go to them and show up for them, not out of pity or with a plan but with a prayerful posture that shows them the real Jesus. This is how I came to know Jesus in a deeper way for three years while not belonging to an organized church community. People who loved me were around me and willing to give me biblically sound resources as well as a listening ear. Not everyone around me did this or did it well, but some did, and I've been forever changed because of it.

Prevention

In my master's program in social work at Nyack College, I learned about preventative measures. They are structures, policies, and systems that prevent certain things from happening or resulting. Now, obviously we cannot prevent everything, but if we don't try at all, our actions show a lack of heart for the world.

Preventative measures show we care about people and want to honor God with what he has given us. Prevention work is also trauma informed because it considers what people have gone through, how we don't want to repeat those experiences, and what has and hasn't worked before.

In the church, we get to implement preventative measures for weariness, wounds, and wandering to become less and less frequent (and in Jesus's name, disappear altogether). The following suggestions are for a church setting but can apply to ministries and other Christian spaces as well (like friendships, conferences, and everyday life).

Prevention for Weariness

- Create opportunities for growth for both new believers and seasoned believers.

- Address what's going on in the Christian world and help people understand that the Bible says scandals, trials, and disappointments will happen. Acting as if such things are not happening can make people feel like they're the only ones noticing or caring. Provide guidance on how to stay encouraged in the midst of these disappointments.
- Evaluate your church and shift things if women need to be more amplified or men need to be better/more discipled. Consider whether a lack of diversity needs to be addressed or living justly needs to become more of a priority. Create better systems and schedules for people serving so no one serves every week or too much. Evaluations help us see what's not healthy and help us humbly acknowledge it.
- Consider restructuring the church budget to spend less on lights, fog machines, exorbitant pastors' salaries, and church aesthetics and more on serving the church community, emergency needs, and local partnerships.
- Actively do what the Bible says. Get involved in civic engagement, care for the marginalized, speak against evil, and do all the other things Jesus touches on in his earthly ministry.
- Be committed to eliminating celebrity culture, not just in your own space but in the collective Christian Body.

Prevention for Wounds

- Ensure there are elders in the church or leaders who are not yes people but rather biblically sound people who are mature and wise enough to address abuse or trauma.
- Don't center the church on one pastor or person.

- Train ministry leaders in biblical leadership, discipleship, gentleness, and communication.
- Create healthy structures that include appropriate amounts of serving hours/time, reevaluation/feedback moments, and member-to-leadership access for support and presence.
- Develop abuse policies and procedures for reporting and repenting, not when something happens but before, even if you think your church is healthy.
- Disciple church members on how to show up for people experiencing struggle, pain, and trauma so they can be the Body well in the world but also to ensure that if someone in the church encounters abuse, people in it are equipped to show up for the victims and others who are wounded.

Prevention for Wandering

- Be a soft, authentic, safe, transparent, gentle, loving, welcoming, truthful, peaceful, grace-filled person with the people of God.
- Teach sound doctrine with biblical evidence and references.
- Show people how to discern God's truth and how other perspectives pervert, change, or distort that truth.
- Address legalism if it's showing up in your church.
- Confront nonbiblical theology if it's showing up in your church.

The weary, wounded, and wandering aren't looking for something that's unattainable. They are just looking for the Radical called Christ and for the church to be him here on earth, as it is in heaven.

RADICAL THOUGHTS

> The weary, wounded, and wandering are our collective responsibility even if we don't identify as any of them or feel we have done anything to cause any of those groups. We are one Body.

> Weariness is something not to shame people for but to encourage people through.

> The wounded are image bearers and not just victims.

> We have all deconstructed at some point.

> The preventative ideas in this chapter are intervention tools too.

REFLECTIVE QUESTIONS

> When's the last time you had a conversation with someone who kept mentioning how tired or over the church they are?

> How have you served those who have been wounded within the church?

> Have you ignored the problems in your church because they aren't personally affecting you?

> Do you feel safe bringing preventative measures to church leadership?

> How can you be a part of the collective restoration?

RESTORATIVE MEDITATION

INHALE: Father, forgive us for overlooking these issues.

EXHALE: Holy Spirit, give us the wisdom to serve people well and help them heal.

INHALE: Lord, we have lost our way.
EXHALE: Redirect our steps and lead us to your restoration.

INHALE: Jesus, we thank you for faithful churches and shepherds.
EXHALE: We pray that healthy churches would outshine the unhealthy ones.

REMAIN IN SCRIPTURE

- Isaiah 40:28
- Matthew 28:19–20
- Acts
- 2 Corinthians 1:3–5
- 1 and 2 Timothy
- Titus

7

Living in Sighs and Silence

> One of the goals of the whole business of liberation was to make it possible for us not to be silenced.
>
> —Toni Morrison[1]

> Fools find no pleasure in understanding
> but delight in airing their own opinions.
>
> —Proverbs 18:2

We've talked about selah and the call to be silent before God, but this chapter is about *being* silenced. Choosing to be silent to listen to God and being silenced by people who claim to love God are two completely different experiences.

On a beautiful fall day in New York City in 2016, I walked into a staff meeting to discuss the winter and early spring schedule.

If you know me, then you know I love this kind of stuff—planning, scheduling, organizing, and so on. But in that season, it wasn't a joyful experience, because none of our thoughts, ideas, or opinions would matter or be included. I knew what I was walking into, just like the rest of the staff did, because it was always the same: it would be a meeting in which we were *told*, not asked, what we would be doing in the coming months.

Eventually, we got to the part of the agenda that concerned December. And, ya'll, I LOVE CHRISTMAS, so I was READYYYYY to be a part of all the Christmas plans. Even in the spiritually abusive situation I was in, I felt a little bit of joy as we were about to talk about Christmas. And then our boss said it: "The Christmas service will be at 7 p.m. on December 24."

Some of you are probably thinking, Girl, what's the problem, shouldn't you want to be in church on the 24th? Well, yes, but here's the thing—we Dominicans (and Latinos/as in general) celebrate something called Noche Buena. It's December 24. If you ask me to do something on December 25, I'll gladly do it because my family and I are not doing a thing on that day. But December 24? Oh, that's our Christmas. And 7 p.m.? Well, that's our start time. The issue here was a lack of awareness of the community, since the church was in Harlem and much of the population in that neighborhood and church included Latinos/as. The other issue was the church's lack of compassion for the already-overworked staff who weren't from town and would therefore be separated from family for Christmas.

As I sat in the meeting and heard this news, I stayed silent.

The phrase "being a voice for the voiceless" communicates that there are people who don't have the thoughts or power to speak. But that's not always true. Oftentimes, people who are considered voiceless have been silenced, oppressed, and abused by people in power. Therefore, our voices feel far from something we can use to defend ourselves or to communicate our thoughts. So I stayed silent. Why? Because in the past I hadn't, and when I had spoken, I had been manipulated, shamed, and targeted. Silence felt safer.

I spent the weeks after that trying to figure out how I would tell my family why I wouldn't be at Noche Buena dinner. Noche Buena means "good night," in the sense that something good happened the night of December 24. On that day, we remember and celebrate the gift God gave us by sending us a Savior. Something that was good quickly became something I couldn't be a part of because I was on staff at a church that didn't understand its community.

The service didn't affect just me. It affected the rest of the Latino/a community that was a part of that church and had to figure out what to choose on December 24—blood family or blood of Christ family. It also affected all the staff who were not native New Yorkers and wanted to go home for the holidays but couldn't.

Our decisions are never just about us—which is why so much of what we do in life should be centered on conversations before decisions are even considered. We didn't walk into a conversation-centered meeting that day; we walked into a meeting with a lead pastor who was the youngest son in his family and probably never felt heard while growing up. So in turn, instead of empathizing with the voiceless, he became the oppressor who silenced others. Scripture tells shepherds to do the opposite in 1 Peter 5:2–4: "Be shepherds of God's flock that is under your care, watching over them—not because you must, but because you are willing, as God wants you to be; not pursuing dishonest gain, but eager to serve; not lording it over those entrusted to you, but being examples to the flock. And when the Chief Shepherd appears, you will receive the crown of glory that will never fade away."

After that Christmas service, we cleaned up the church while the pastors left and went home to join their families. They said, "Enjoy your week break," as if a week off could heal our spiritual weariness, physical exhaustion, and mental stretch from another year of working in a church that didn't see us, honor us, or value us. As soon as we were done, I got an Uber (which took a long time because, duh, it was Christmas Eve) and other staff headed straight to the airport to get on their overpriced flights because working on December 24 had been required of all of us.

Our decisions should be conversations because when they aren't, someone is being silenced. But our decisions shouldn't be just conversations; they should also come from a place of awareness. This church was located in a neighborhood that was 43 percent Black (which can account for Black Latinos/as like me) and 37 percent Latino/a. The church was also full of transplants to New York City—people who didn't grow up in New York City and didn't have family there.

Pastors need awareness but so does the collective Body of Christ. We need awareness in our homes, our workplaces, our families, and our neighborhoods. We are close to certain people for a reason, and our role is not to make them become like us but to allow them to influence us in a positive way. When we try to make them become like us, we silence who they are.

Overall, this church's leaders weren't interested in learning about or acknowledging the history of the people of color of

New York City. They wanted a Christmas service, an event, instead of space for people's circumstances, cultures, and cares. The church silenced people, and that is not the way of the radical and certainly not the trauma-informed path.

A Code of Silence

I had begun working at this church shortly before this Christmas service situation. At my first meeting with the church leadership, they told me not to talk to my husband about anything bad or negative I might experience at the church because it could affect my husband's faith. That was the beginning of my silencing—my first day of work at a church. And guess what I did? I was silent for almost a year. Why? Because I was taught that verses like this one have no exceptions and apply to all shepherds: "Have confidence in your leaders and submit to their authority, because they keep watch over you as those who must give an account. Do this so that their work will be a joy, not a burden, for that would be of no benefit to you" (Heb. 13:17). But not every person who holds the position of pastor is an actual shepherd.

I was a baby Christian when I went to work at this church, and in many ways I feel that my lack of biblical literacy was weaponized against me. I experienced spiritual abuse, manipulation, silencing, racism, disrespect, unethical salary practices, burnout, and so much more. One day I finally decided to listen to the Holy Spirit, who said, "Something's not right." I reflected and prayed and talked to my husband. He was in shock about everything I told him, and he was also angry (not at me) that I hadn't told him any of it for almost a year. We decided to leave the church. I share elements of this story because (1) I know many people will relate to it, and I want you to know you're not alone, and (2) I want those of you who are a part of a church to consider the ways you can pay attention and notice when people are being silenced and how God wants you to address a silencing pattern.

Erasing, Tokenizing, and Silencing Image Bearers

I've seen many of these same dynamics in stories people have shared with me, in the news, and through simple observation. We discussed the doctrine of discovery in the chapter on uniformity. Now let's talk about how that doctrine perpetuates the narrative of Whiteness being the foundational culture of the church. Before we keep going, it's important that we acknowledge that talking about Whiteness goes beyond just talking about White people. As we've established, no group is monolithic. Whiteness, historically—especially in the United States—means that White culture, language, and way of living and being have been seen as the primary example for all people and circumstances. This doesn't mean that every White person is projecting themselves onto others, but it does mean that the culture of Whiteness is not just predominant but expected and the norm in the United States, and in the church.

One of the primary goals of Whiteness is to remain the dominant culture, people, and narrator. This has often resulted in other people being erased or tokenized, which ultimately leads to them being silenced. If you're trying to erase me, then you're silencing my voice, history, and culture. If you're trying to tokenize me, then you're silencing the millions of other people who come from where I come from, look like me, or sound like me.

How does this show up in Christian culture? Here I'd like to address what silencing looks like to a few specific groups of people.

For Christian people of color within the Body of Christ, silencing looks like the following:

- Having Christian contemporary music—not gospel or *coritos* (Spanish worship music)—be the main kind of music used in conferences and Sunday church services even if the people present are people of color.
- Having a publishing industry that is 90 percent White among staff and authors.
- Having a person of color preach or speak (on your podcast, at your church, to your small group, and so on) only in themed months, such as Black History Month, Latino/a Heritage Month, and Asian American and Pacific Islander History Month.
- Having conferences where one token person of each race or one person of color fulfills an unspoken quota, as if all people of color are the same.
- Having one person of color on staff at a church in a diverse city/town.

For Christians with disabilities within the Body of Christ, silencing looks like the following:

- Not accommodating for wheelchairs, not allowing service dogs, or not having ramps or elevators for people to enter spaces.

- Using lights during a service without considering people who are highly sensitive to bright or moving lights.
- Not having someone on staff or on call who knows sign language if that kind of translation is needed.
- Not having children's programming for children with special needs (or not having staff trained in this area).

For Christians who are women within the Body of Christ, silencing looks like the following:

- Only and always having them be the women's ministry leader and the children's church leader.
- Having events centered on flowers and the book of Esther only.
- Not training the staff of a church on sexual harassment.
- Not discipling the men of the church to grow in maturity as husbands.
- Not believing women who share that they have experienced abuse.

Silencing also occurs for singles, married folks, same-sex-attracted people, people experiencing homelessness, people struggling financially, and people who are put into positions where they aren't heard but instead are told what is good for them and what is better for them. By considering these examples, we can allow the Holy Spirit to convict us in how we have either contributed to these dynamics or allowed them to continue. Silencing happens not just in an organized church community but in ministries, Christian spaces and communities, conferences, podcasts, books, the music industry, and everywhere else Christians find themselves engaged or present.

Contributing to the Health of the Body of Christ

I genuinely believe many Christians want to help end abuse, silencing, and othering within the church but just don't know how. Sometimes to know how to help we first need to understand what we've done or been a part of that hasn't helped. Here's a list of what to avoid or resist that often perpetuates church abuse/trauma/wounds/silencing:

- *Covering the truth*. This is when we know something and either silence the victim or cover the abuser. I have seen this happen time and time again. The story of the evangelist Ravi Zacharias is an example. Several leaders at his ministry, Ravi Zacharias International Ministries, pushed for transparency and accountability when whispers of his abuse started circulating. These leaders wanted the truth to emerge. But other leaders took Zacharias's account at face value, suppressed the truth, and labeled questioning staff members as disloyal or unchristian. The news about Zacharias rocked me a bit, especially because when we all found out we were already going through hard things in 2020. But our faith is in Christ and not a person. And Christ is the truth, which means we should always be ready and willing to tell the truth with wisdom and gentleness.
- *Failing to confront*. Most people in power who abuse can do so because they're surrounded by yes people. When we look at the life of Jesus and his relationship with the disciples, we see him as someone who was willing to have difficult conversations. If you feel you can't confront the person doing the abusing, that's a red flag.

- *Tribalism*. One of the biggest threats to the church in the United States is that we are not one Body. Instead, we are many little bodies. We are tribes. We have become so committed to our specific church that we're willing to protect it and the unhealthy things happening within it. Being invested in the local church is good, but a local church is a finger in the bigger Body. If the finger is unhealthy, the whole Body is affected. Tribalism also happens when a church is centered on one person or pastor, which then perpetuates celebrity culture.
- *Self-centered mindset*. When people raise concerns about an abusive leader, we respond with rationales like "But he is nice to me" or "But she really helped me." We think that because we've had a positive experience, others can't have a negative experience. No one is completely evil, and we aren't dismissing the good the person has done, but would we ever go to Jesus when we've sinned and say, "But, Lord, I helped that family yesterday" or "But, God, I've been committed to discipling this person"? Good actions don't erase bad ones. We have to address the harm someone has done even if they have done good. Both can coexist.
- *Disbelief*. We need to be more intentional about believing people when they raise concerns or speak of their church wounds. Do people lie? Certainly, but our heart posture should be that we believe people first and ask the Holy Spirit to give us discernment. Disbelief is one of the biggest reasons many people don't return to the church. The abuse certainly traumatized them, but not

being believed by people who claimed to love them is oftentimes a worse kind of pain.

- *Lack of perspective*. We'll talk more about justice in part 3 of this book, but as the Body of Christ, we need to see abuse and trauma in the church as an injustice issue. Because we don't know what category to put church trauma and abuse in, we often don't do anything about them. But people are being dehumanized. That's injustice.
- *Grace without truth*. If we look at the comments section of a post by a Christian leader who has "fallen" and apologized, we often see a flood of comments from people (who likely don't personally know this person) saying that they love them and support them all the way. Grace is magnified, and truth dismissed. This means we are so focused on extending grace to someone who has sinned that we overlook accountability, recovery, and repentance. Anyone can post an apology on Instagram. The harder work is to repent, step down, take time to grow, or take other actions.

If you've been silenced, abused, or traumatized by someone in the Body of Christ or you're a friend of someone who has been, here are some things that may help with healing:

- *Address your pain, hurt, and trauma*. When I first left a spiritual abuse situation, I just tried to move on to another church. That didn't help because I just ended up in a similar situation. What has helped is addressing what I went through with the help of therapy, books, community, prayer, forgiveness, time, journaling, decolonizing my view of church, deconstructing the truth of Christ, and naming what I went through. We must face the trauma rather than hide from it.

- *Spend time with trusted and safe Christians.* Just because someone is a Christian doesn't mean they are a safe person. In trying to heal, we need to discern who is actually safe and who can actually handle our story.
- *Learn healing tools and the effects of trauma.* Many books and programs specialize in teaching people about trauma. The more we know about it, the more we can understand how it's affecting our whole selves.
- *Pray.* This can look different than it has before, because perhaps the thing you went through in a church setting or with Christians was manipulation or misuse of prayer. Sometimes prayer can just be a few words or repeating Scripture we love. Live liberated, knowing that prayer is a conversation with your Father.

Let's close by reviewing both unhelpful ways to be with people who are wounded or weary because of the church and helpful and healthy ways to proceed:

- I've heard many people say something like this: "If you don't like a restaurant, just don't go to that one. If you don't like a church, just don't go to it." Those are completely different things and shouldn't be compared. Saying this dismisses the experiences a person had at a church. Instead, be the church for that person by showing up for them in their pain and weariness. Do not let them stay there forever, but do not rush them out of that place.

- Saying "I know you went through that, *but* not every place is the same" may be completely true, but it is still dismissive. Instead, ask the person if they've had a good experience with a church or a Christian and what made it good. From there, explore the idea that they might find good in another church when they're ready to search for one.
- Do not say, "I know they hurt you, but they aren't completely bad" or "They really helped me." Friend, with all the love in the world, I want to say it's not about you. It's about a person who went through a difficult thing. It may very well be true that the person who abused your friend was good to you or that they aren't a completely bad person, but that isn't what someone who is suffering needs to hear as they heal. Refer to chapter 5 for more examples of how to be a trauma-informed person to others who are suffering.
- If a person is suffering, just be with them. Be their friend. Be Jesus's hands and feet. Don't try to be their savior or even their pastor. They need a friend more than anything. Try to understand their pain and weariness and be present with them there. Most people just need a friend, and they need to know the Body of Christ hasn't fully abandoned them.
- Don't rush a person back to church. I often told people in my healing and deconstructing journey that my goal was ultimately to be a part of a healthy church. Some people think that if a person takes a few years to heal

> they don't intend on being a part of a church at all anymore. But that's just not true. They are just taking their time. If someone is single for a while, we don't assume they want to be single forever. We might assume they are taking their time to find someone of value. The same applies to those who want to return to church but not go through the same things again. Healthy churches exist, but they aren't the easiest thing to find.

Many of us sigh at all that's been going on in the church. Sometimes it feels like we don't even have the words to express what we really think and feel about it all. That's perhaps why we sigh in the first place. It's the only expression we have that really conveys what we feel. Friend, I understand. It's important to know that it's okay to sigh and be disappointed with the church. But it's also important we stay hopeful and contribute to the restoration of the Body of Christ. It's not okay that you have been silenced, and I'm sorry if you have been. It's not okay that others have been silenced either. My hope is that resources like this one land in the hands of people willing to break the silence and amplify the voices of the forgotten, silenced, overlooked, and othered in the global church.

RADICAL THOUGHTS

- The church is not broken, but it is bruised.
- The healing of the church will come through everyday radicals willing to have hard conversations, speak truth to power, and advocate for the silenced.
- We don't have to get used to church abuse stories. They are not normal, and we can make them a rare thing if we try.

- The silenced should be most heard within the church.
- Sighing doesn't mean you don't love the church. It means you love her enough to want her to change.

REFLECTIVE QUESTIONS

- Have you helped to perpetuate abuse in the church?
- What can you do in your everyday life to advocate for the silenced?
- How have you silenced people's cultures and experiences?
- What can you do to be a better listener to the marginalized?
- How can your everyday life shift so you can include the silenced and invite them into your life, church, experiences, and so on?

RESTORATIVE MEDITATION

INHALE: El Roi, we thank you for seeing the silenced.
EXHALE: Help us see the ones we've ignored.

INHALE: Holy Spirit, thank you for giving value to our voices.
EXHALE: May we be people who invite all voices to the house of God.

INHALE: We praise you for intentionally making such a unique humanity.
EXHALE: Forgive us for not embracing that more and guide us to your radical way.

REMAIN IN SCRIPTURE

- Proverbs 18:2
- Matthew 7:14
- 1 Timothy 6:3–5
- Hebrews 13:17
- 1 Peter 5:2–4

8

Souls over Sides and Stances

> When two brothers are busy fighting, an evil man can easily attack and rob their poor mother. Mankind should always stay united, standing shoulder to shoulder so evil can never cheat and divide them.
>
> —Suzy Kassem, *Rise Up and Salute the Sun*[1]

> Jesus knew their thoughts and said to them: "Any kingdom divided against itself will be ruined, and a house divided against itself will fall."
>
> —Luke 11:17

There is a day in history that many of us will always remember. Most of us probably started it by getting ready for work or school or attending to our kiddos. It was a Monday, so perhaps some of us were grieving that the weekend was officially over, while the optimistic among us were excited for what the week would bring. It was Three Kings Day. If you are Latino/a/Hispanic, then you know what that means. We as a community celebrate that day, which coincides with Epiphany.

On that day, a group of thousands of people, many of whom claim to follow Jesus, gathered. This gathering included prayer, the Bible, and signs with the name of Jesus on them in big, bold, red, capital letters. This gathering had been planned for a while, and planned well. It had one common stance and one common goal.

The gathering caught most of us off guard, but by the end of the day, it wasn't really that surprising (at least not to me). It created a commotion, ignited feelings, and was a first of its kind.

I'm talking about January 6, 2021, when thousands of people stormed the US Capitol in Washington, DC. AP News published images of people holding Bibles and Trump signs. Religion News Service published images of participants holding hands and apparently praying to Jesus inside the chamber of the Capitol. One Religion News Service article reported that "one of the insurrectionists perched atop the Senate desk paused to shout 'Jesus Christ, we invoke your name!'"[2] *Sojourners* reported that some people storming the Capitol did so while shouting, "Jesus is my Savior, Trump is my president!" alongside people holding signs that said, "In God We Trust" and "Jesus Saves."[3]

Why does this matter? First, many of the people at the insurrection weren't just Trump supporters or Republicans. They were people who claimed to love and follow Jesus and represent him in public. Although most Christians might think, "They're not really Christian," the world and many of our neighbors said, "Yup, there go those Christians." We are one Body, so what others do affects the Body and the representation of Jesus to the world.

Second, it matters because it reminds us that following Jesus isn't just a simple matter of praying the sinner's prayer. No, it's a sanctified life that is devoted to the way and teachings of Jesus. We will always fall short of this, but our effort is the fruit of being bold enough to follow him. The number of people who claim to be Christian who attended the January 6 insurrection reveals a deep disconnect between what we know about the Bible and how we live out what the Bible actually says.

Third, it matters because, despite their illegal and un-Christlike behavior, every single person who showed up on January 6 is an image bearer who deserves dignity. I'm not saying they shouldn't face consequences or that we should ignore what they did. What I'm saying is that we get to choose souls before stances and sides. As a person of color who witnessed the person the January 6 rioters were supporting (Trump) talk about people in my gender, racial, and cultural group in a way that makes us seem like less than human, I feel strong feelings about that day and what those people think of me and my humanity. Naturally, this makes me want to take a stance or side against them. And perhaps it is wise and Christlike to do so because of what they represent, what they did, and how they did it. Yet, what we sometimes do with our stances and sides is forget souls. I don't agree with them or support them. I don't plan on making a fan page about them either. I actually rebuke their actions, but I still need to honor who they are as image bearers when I talk about them and think about them or if I ever meet them. Even when Jesus corrected and rebuked, he did not forget the soul to which he was speaking. He didn't forget their dignity and humanity, and neither should we.

Stances and sides without consideration of souls creates wars, division, dehumanization, castes, and many other terrible things that prevent peace, healthy humanity, or love. I gave you this extreme example of January 6 because we struggle to love people (especially online) who have even the slightest difference of opinion. If we struggle to love them, how can we love and honor the rioter or the racist? Remember what I mean by love. Love doesn't mean affirmation or allowance of dishonor or dehumanization. Love is much more than that.

A stance is a standpoint or an attitude of a person or organization about something. We can absolutely have healthy stances, so I'm not telling you to never have a stance on anything. That would make you indifferent or passive. But on things that are divisive, sensitive, or controversial, your stance shouldn't trump the honor and dignity you have for the person who has a different stance. It's just not the way of the radical. Our stances and sides, if we let them, can convince us that we have a right to dehumanize others—that's what oppression has always done. But seeing souls makes room for what Jesus did: correct with both truth and grace and extend compassion at all times.

For example, I believe women can preach anywhere and to anyone. Millions of other Christians disagree with me and have a different stance on this issue. Should I be canceled or disrespected because we have different interpretations? Should I assume those who disagree with me are ignorant or have no biblical literacy or are sexist? No. Although I'm sure some people who believe women should not preach are sexist, I don't believe that is every person's foundation for interpreting Paul's teachings on gender and the church.

This same narrative applies to sides. In the November 2022 election in New York City, I did not vote for the Senate candidate that most people thought I would vote for. I didn't take the side that everyone around me was taking. I went a different route, and although I do love to cause a little ruckus occasionally, I didn't publicize who I voted for because, honey, that's my business. But by voting, I ultimately did take a side, and I didn't have to ridicule, judge, or dishonor people who took a different side than I did. Just like with stances, there are some positive aspects to picking a side. For example, every time a person has come to me with their church wound story, I have believed them, and by believing them, I have taken their side because in this lifetime I will never take the side of an oppressor or abuser. Yet I will not dishonor or disrespect an oppressor or abuser because they have a soul and are an image bearer of God. I will hold them accountable, though.

This idea always reminds me of Psalm 8:4, which says, "What is mankind that you are mindful of them, human beings that you care for them?" God is mindful of *all* of us. The oppressor and the oppressed. The abuser and the abused. The lost and the found. The sinner and the saint. The atheist and the Christian. The old and the young. The quiet and the loud. The follower and the leader. The fearful and the bold. The pastor and the new Christian. The apostle and the apostate. He is mindful of all of us, and his mindfulness gives us dignity.

When Jesus says love God and love others, he's not saying love God when it's easy and love only those who look like you and agree with you. No, he is saying love God and others unconditionally and without excuse.

In this chapter, we are going to look at a few timely topics that create division in the church.

Critical Race Theory

Yeah, let's go there, friends. As a social worker, I learned about critical race theory in my master's and PhD programs, so when I started to see so many people in the church screaming (not talking) about it a few years ago, I was highly confused. That's the thing about a divisive virus. Once it hits a few people, it spreads quickly, even though people don't even know what it is.

So what is critical race theory? Here's one definition from a credible source:

> Critical race theory (CRT) [is an] intellectual and social movement and loosely organized framework of legal analysis based on the premise that race is not a natural, biologically grounded feature of physically distinct subgroups of human beings but a socially constructed (culturally invented) category that is used to oppress and exploit people of color. Critical race theorists hold that racism is inherent in the law and legal institutions of the United States insofar as they function to create and maintain social, economic, and political inequalities between whites and nonwhites, especially African Americans. Critical race theorists are generally dedicated to applying their understanding of the institutional or structural nature of racism to the concrete (if distant) goal of eliminating all race-based and other unjust hierarchies.[4]

So many of us are proud of our race, but, especially before colonization, many of us belonged not to a race but to an ethnicity. Even some ethnicities have been invented because of colonization. For example, I am Dominican, and our good ol' pal Christopher Columbus (the rapist, colonizer, racist, enslaver, and murderer) landed on the island of Hispaniola (which is the

Dominican Republic and Haiti together) on his first voyage in 1492. This means that before 1492, there were no Dominicans, because that name for our ethnicity was given later. So my ethnic group is about five hundred years old. Some in my ethnic group consider themselves Black and some don't. Race was culturally invented with a very specific agenda that began with the discovery of the Americas. Periodt, with a t. It's not a coincidence that the time colonizers started naming groups of people based on their skin tone (race) was also around the time they began the transatlantic slave trade. How convenient.

I'm not trying to convince you to support or engage with CRT. What I am saying is that we are fighting against these challenging, confusing, and complex ideas because (drumroll, please) . . . they are uncomfortable.

They are uncomfortable for White people, whose ancestors invented a racialized hierarchy for their own advancement. They're uncomfortable for people of color, who were given race names based on their skin tone and region of ancestry. Talking about race is uncomfortable, especially in a country like the United States, which has a complicated, at times horrendous, history with race. But don't worry. We aren't the only ones. Plenty of people throughout the world have difficulty talking about race. I don't know who is doing it best, so perhaps we can simply go to Jesus.

Every time one of his disciples or someone mentioned an ethnic group of people in a negative, oppressive, or dishonorable way, Jesus had something to say about it and responded respectfully but also directly, with the aim of always dignifying who was being spoken about in a dehumanizing way and who was doing the disrespectful talking. Both/and.

This is where the parable of the good Samaritan comes into play. We'll talk more about this powerful story later, but for now, let's highlight that Jesus is talking to the Jewish community when he tells this story, and he is talking about a Samaritan who exemplifies what Jesus wants to teach. Jewish people thought very poorly of Samaritans. Jesus invites them to consider not just the beaten man on the road, the Levite and priest who pass by the beaten man, and the robbers who hurt him but also someone they consider ungodly, dirty, and not worthy of dignity. Jesus says they do have dignity, and so much so that their dignity translates into love for the least, lost, and beaten. If Jews were to choose the stance of their people or the side of pride, they would lose sight of the beautiful soul found in the Samaritan. CRT doesn't have to be a side or a stance to fight against within the church. What if it was simply a conversation?

LGBTQIA+

In November 2022, I spoke at a conference, and after it ended, after everyone had left and the team was cleaning up, I was sitting in the lobby when someone came up to me and said, "I have never heard a Christian talk from a stage about what I previously identified as and went through with gender dysphoria with such truth and grace." We went on to have a beautiful conversation, and we both ended up crying. After the person left, I went into the sanctuary and kept crying. There were two reasons for this. One, I was honored that God had spoken through me in a way that ministered to that person and helped them be seen by God. And two, I was heartbroken that I was the first Christian they had heard speak graciously about them from a stage.

That same November, just a few days before Thanksgiving, there was a mass shooting in a gay club in Colorado Springs. Here are things I heard people say in the aftermath:

"There is a consequence for how we sin."
"If you're non-affirming, then you're just as responsible as the person who was holding that gun."
"They didn't deserve that, but they should stop living that way."
"Non-affirming Christians should be quiet in times like these."

What were these statements really communicating? "I'm choosing the 'right' side of things, and so my stance is biblical." But the only biblical stance regarding the murder of people is grief, lament, mourning, peace, comfort, and honor. None of those statements communicated any of those things.

If grief and honor are absent of dignity, they become disrespectful and dehumanizing.

One of the biggest ways the enemy is separating the church today is by convincing us that our stances must develop into sides and that these sides must mean opposing groups that won't listen to one another. But no human body should live divided. Mark 3:24–26 says, "If a kingdom is divided against itself, that kingdom cannot stand. If a house is divided against itself, that house cannot stand. And if Satan opposes himself and is divided, he cannot stand; his end has come."

What if we chose to fight the enemy by showing dignity and respect to each other even in the midst of disagreement? How much more could we conquer evil and heal what has been broken? How much more functional and healthy would our churches be?

The LGBTQIA+ community is not a monolithic group of people who are to be exiled and judged. Rather, they should be loved and seen. Walked with and cared for. Covered and protected. Ministered to and prayed for. They are not a project to fix. If they love and claim to follow Jesus, they are within the Body, and if they don't, they are still image bearers. Either way, dignity gets to be the portion we pour out to them, not because we affirm or don't affirm but because we accept the call from God to love God and others. I'm not saying that we shouldn't address sin or encourage repentance. I'm saying that we should love the person while not letting our sides or stances get in the way. Otherwise we will have become legalistic Pharisees who want to enforce more than invite. We have seen how the church historically has taken sides and stances to harm this community, making them want nothing to do with God. And that should break our hearts enough to change not our biblical interpretations but our approach to loving others well.

Cliques

The final area of sides and stances I want to address is the development of division by way of cliques within organized church communities. This kind of division is, I think, the worst of them because it makes us arrogant, proud, and divisive. You will never find me describing Christians (or even myself) with an umbrella term like *progressive*, *conservative*, *liberal*, *egalitarian*, *complementarian*, or *woke*. People will often ask me, "How did you end up being friends with that conservative group of people?" or when I'm going to preach where both men and women will be present, they ask, "Aren't you complementarian?" Whatever happened to just having conversations? I've been working on my speaker list for my next conference, and I've been asking the women how they feel about preaching to men and women. I'm not assuming (unless they have publicly communicated their feelings). There's a difference between a person saying they are a conservative and you saying they are because of your assumptions. Assumptions put people on sides they may not even be on.

Divisions also happen when people want to be around only people who have the same theology or perspective as they do. Don't misunderstand. There's nothing wrong with wanting to be around people you have things in common with, but in the church we all have the common ground of being followers of Jesus, children of God, and temples of the Holy Spirit. Any other commonality is just extra. On top of that, if everyone around us thinks the same way we do, we are limiting our growth and the opportunity to learn from other sides and stances, which will lead us less and less to see the soul of a person when we meet someone different from us at church or in Christian spaces.

There's also a type of clique that has access to the pastor, not because the pastor is discipling people (which would be a reason for closeness) but because the pastor has created an exclusive group that gets exclusive access and information. I've been a part of three churches where this happened, and in two of those churches I was a part of the "in" pastor group. It's truly so unhealthy. If the leaders of a church create cliques, a church culture of exclusivity trickles down to members of the church, who then create their own cliques.

Putting Souls before Stances and Sides

As the Body, what does it mean and look like to put souls before stances and sides?

Let's look at what Jesus says. In Matthew 22, someone asks Jesus a question and he responds. A similar interaction is found in Luke 10. Scholars can't decide (or agree on) if Matthew 22 and Luke 10 describe the same interaction, but based on the person

Jesus is talking to and what Jesus says, let's assume they do. In both cases, Jesus is talking to an expert in the law—a Pharisee or Sadducee—and they would already have known the answer to the question they ask. In Luke 10:25, they ask, "Teacher, . . . what must I do to inherit eternal life?" In Matthew 22:36, they ask, "Teacher, which is the greatest commandment in the Law?"

Both times Scripture says the same thing.

In Luke 10:27, Jesus says, "'Love the Lord your God with all your heart and with all your soul and with all your strength and with all your mind'; and, 'Love your neighbor as yourself.'" And in Matthew 22:37–40, he says, "'Love the Lord your God with all your heart and with all your soul and with all your mind.' This is the first and greatest commandment. And the second is like it: 'Love your neighbor as yourself.' All the Law and the Prophets hang on these two commandments."

Both instances include a person who knows God's Word (by memory) and knows these answers because they are found in Deuteronomy 6:5 and Leviticus 19:18. That's us. We are the Pharisees and Sadducees asking God the question we already know the answer to.

How do we dignify others?
How do we love others well?
How do we focus on souls over stances and sides?
How do we break the sin of divisiveness in the Body?
How can we be the Body well?

We have the answers, friends. All sixty-six books of the Bible tell us the answers, so really this book is just an affirming conviction. I'm not saying new things or innovative things. I'm reiterating what Jesus already said. But many of us do feel we have to ask again, so I hope that as you ask these questions, you will find the answers in this book and that the answers will stir up action and ignite a deep conviction in your heart. Because if we just know God's Word and don't live it out, we won't be the Body.

The world is in desperate need of the Body. Millions of souls are waiting for us to show up with grace in our hearts, peace in our minds, and truth coming out of our mouths with graciousness, gentleness, and godliness. We need to show up.

For the seventeen-year-old leaving the church like I did.

For the thirty-four-year-old deconstructing and confused.

For the fifty-eight-year-old who grew up in the church and left a long time ago.

For the two-year-old who has the potential to be a part of a healthy Christian generation in the future.

For the ten-year-old who loves God but is confused by those who claim to love them.

For the lost and the found and the weary and the wandering and the hopeless.

That is whom we get to show up for. Whom we get to be soft for. For the glory of God.

May we live out the way of the radical and choose souls over stances and sides every single time.

RADICAL THOUGHTS

- Being soft with others doesn't mean affirming sin.
- Who people vote for is not a salvation issue.
- Racism is taught, which means it can be unlearned.
- Every soul matters to God more than stances and sides.

REFLECTIVE QUESTIONS

> How do we dignify others?

> How do we love others well?

> How do we focus on souls over stances and sides?

> How do we break the sin of divisiveness in the Body?

> How can we be the Body well?

> What are your political views, and have they gotten in the way of how you see and treat others who vote differently?

> Do you have a relationship with somebody who identifies as LGBTQIA+? If not, why not? Have you excluded this group of people from your life?

> If you're Reformed, is everyone around you Reformed too? Do you have Christian friends who have different theological perspectives?

> How can you be soft by choosing souls over everything else?

RESTORATIVE MEDITATION

INHALE: Lord of unity and dignity,
EXHALE: we exalt you and want to follow you and your ways alone.

INHALE: We ask for forgiveness for the ways we have chosen stances and sides.
EXHALE: May we be people who choose souls, just as you choose them daily.

INHALE: Lord of armies, help us in this battle of divisiveness within the Body of Christ.
EXHALE: We need restoration and redemption.

REMAIN IN SCRIPTURE

- o Psalm 8:4
- o Matthew 22:37–40
- o Mark 3:24–26
- o Luke 10:27
- o Luke 11:17
- o 1 Corinthians 1:10–13

Choosing to Be Last

But many who are first will be last,
and many who are last will be first.
—Matthew 19:30

There is a people.

A people God has invited to be last.

Who will choose the humble walk of being forgotten if Christ be remembered.

Who will consider compassion to be much more than just being nice, more like a radical act of seeing other image bearers with the eyes of God and as a result treating them as such.

Who will not casually witness injustice globally and locally and repost about it as mission accomplished.

Who will choose to be last not with the goal of trying to be first.

Who will see the cross as a convicting reminder that instead of being last, we could have remained lost.

Who will not casually walk this earth with the most powerful message of all and stay silent.

Will we be the last?

The Body of Christ.

Sanctuaries.

Safe houses.

Sanctified.

Laboring as the last for the lost and loved.

PART 3

Safe—From Observing to Responding

Never forget that justice is what love looks like in public.

—Cornel West

9

Know Peace, Know Justice

> Injustice anywhere is a threat to justice everywhere. We are caught in an inescapable network of mutuality, tied in a single garment of destiny. Whatever affects one directly, affects all indirectly.
>
> —Martin Luther King Jr.[1]

> Finally, brothers and sisters, rejoice! Strive for full restoration, encourage one another, be of one mind, live in peace. And the God of love and peace will be with you.
>
> —2 Corinthians 13:11

Have you ever heard the chant "No justice, no peace"? This is often shouted by people who are fed up with the injustices they see, particularly in the United States. It communicates that if people don't get justice and aren't treated with dignity, then there will be no peace. Sometimes this means that a lack of justice results in social disruption and divides. Sometimes it communicates that if there's no justice, then people will act in ways that are anything but peaceful.

This response to the consistent and continuous murdering of Black bodies and being expected to move on from mass shootings in elementary schools is an understandable one. But we have another, better way and response.

In the next few chapters, we'll explore how to be a justice-centered Body of Christ. Because *justice* has become a trendy word, we seem to have lost sight of what it actually means, but Jesus and his Word direct us well in what it can mean in our everyday lives. The world is in need of justice and justice workers—and that's us.

Sometimes I am asked, "What led you to have a heart for justice?" and my response is always the same: "Because Jesus cares about justice and is a justice worker himself." Most people assume I'm for justice and speak on it often because I'm a woman of color and a daughter of immigrants, because I have lived and currently live where marginalized people reside, and because I have personally experienced injustice. But if those were my reasons for caring about justice, then my work would be about my feelings and lived experience. They would be an excuse for those who don't share my story to not care about justice. But Jesus calls us to a radical way. He calls us to have a heart for justice because he does. He invites us to care about things not solely based on our experiences but because he cares about them. Thankfully, he doesn't leave us to guess what he thinks about injustice. It's apparent throughout the Scriptures.

In this chapter, we'll start with the basics—to know peace and then as a result to know what justice looks like.

Justice is Right Side Up

My sister (in Christ) Yana Jenay, a theologian, Bible teacher, and writer, notes that Christians often talk about Jesus's kingdom being upside down. This means that Jesus and Christians aren't of this world, and so the things they do, say, and think seem upside down compared to what the world is thinking, saying, and doing. Yana says, "Jesus's kingdom is right side up, and the kingdom of this world is the one that's upside down. . . . The ways of Jesus help us get the world back to the original design and vision that God had in mind when he created the heavens and the earth."[2]

She goes on to say that our world needs to be turned right side up and refers to the garden in Genesis as a picture of that. She invites us to explore justice from a right-side-up perspective inside the upside-down way the world sees it. We are not to shout, "No justice, no peace," because that way is actually upside-down. We are to live knowing peace and therefore knowing justice. Then by knowing justice, we will live it out, because when we know something, it's not just information to sit in our brains but a tool to activate the good within us to add good to the world. This is the right-side-up path.

But before we can do that, we need to know peace, and Peace is a person. Ephesians 2:14 tells us this: "For he himself is our peace, who has made the two groups one and has destroyed the barrier, the dividing wall of hostility."

Isaiah 9:6 says, "For to us a child is born, to us a son is given, and the government will be on his shoulders. And he will be called Wonderful Counselor, Mighty God, Everlasting Father, Prince of Peace."

Second Thessalonians 3:16 says, "Now may the Lord of peace himself give you peace at all times and in every way. The Lord be with all of you."

And John 14:27 says, "Peace I leave with you; my peace I give you. I do not give to you as the world gives. Do not let your hearts be troubled and do not be afraid."

Jesus himself is both peace and the provider of peace. He is the provider of peace because as the Prince of Peace, he has authority to give it. He is our shalom. He was in the garden as the Word in the beginning, and peace was present there. To know Jesus is to know peace, and to know peace is to know justice. Justice doesn't exist without peace. In other words, justice doesn't exist without Jesus.

But what exactly is justice? Work, words, and living centered on dismantling systems, cultures, structures, and norms that oppress and dehumanize people in order to move toward a collective flourishing.

This description of justice could be Jesus's résumé. This is part of what he came to do and what he continues to do through the Body of Christ. It's important for us to recognize our role in Jesus's restorative work because he's accomplishing shalom, flourishing, and healing from injustice through his church.

The question is, Will we rise up and become responders to injustice?

One of the best examples of how God responds to injustice is found in Exodus 3:7–10:

> The LORD said, "I have indeed seen the misery of my people in Egypt. I have heard them crying out because of their slave driv-

> ers, and I am concerned about their suffering. So I have come down to rescue them from the hand of the Egyptians and to bring them up out of that land into a good and spacious land, a land flowing with milk and honey—the home of the Canaanites, Hittites, Amorites, Perizzites, Hivites and Jebusites. And now the cry of the Israelites has reached me, and I have seen the way the Egyptians are oppressing them. So now, go. I am sending you to Pharaoh to bring my people the Israelites out of Egypt."

Here we see a beautiful picture of God observing injustice and responding to it. We are invited to do the same. To go from being an observing Body of Christ that sees injustice to being an active Body of Christ that responds to injustice. Verse 8 in the passage above says that God came to rescue his people, but he does it through a person. If you know anything about Moses's story, you know he had a crazy childhood that almost left him dead, he murdered someone, and as a result he ran away. This is who God called to free all the Jewish slaves in Egypt—someone who had sinned and who didn't feel qualified.

Justice work isn't comfortable, but if we're willing to say yes to God, then he will go with us into circumstances that seem hopeless, broken, and oppressive.

Exodus 3:1–3 says:

> Now Moses was tending the flock of Jethro his father-in-law, the priest of Midian, and he led the flock to the far side of the wilderness and came to Horeb, the mountain of God. There the angel of the LORD appeared to him in flames of fire from within a bush. Moses saw that though the bush was on fire it

> did not burn up. So Moses thought, "I will go over and see this strange sight—why the bush does not burn up."

Moses was straight chillin'. He was working his job on what was probably just a regular Tuesday. Perhaps he had just finished his lunch when all of a sudden he got an invitation from the Lord. The truth is that he could have just kept his day going as usual. But he didn't just observe a burning bush that stayed intact. He responded by going to the bush. He was already being like Christ. I think we forget that following Christ isn't as complicated as we sometimes make it out to be—especially in the area of injustice. Is it hard sometimes? Absolutely. But if we know Peace, then we can know justice and become responders to injustice. At that moment, Moses didn't know he was responding to a call to be a justice worker, but he would soon find out.

Verse 4 goes on to say, "When the LORD saw that he had gone over to look, God called to him from within the bush, 'Moses! Moses!' And Moses said, 'Here I am.'" God went to Moses, and Moses said, "Here I am."

If you've been looking for a simple way to live more justly, learn more about justice, or understand what it entails, Exodus 3:4 offers an answer. It's simply the willingness to respond to God by saying, "Here I am." Later in chapter 4, Moses hesitates and asks God questions, which is normal, but he still ends up doing what God calls him to do. To free Israel from slavery.

People often don't respond to injustice because it involves being uncomfortable or not knowing what to do, how to do it, or whether it'll be effective. So for the remainder of this chapter, we're going to look at four ways of living justly that can be applied to our everyday lives in tangible ways.

Interceding

In the past few years, we have heard people say no to prayer and yes to action and policy change. I say why not both? Especially if we are followers of Christ, we don't need to choose. Jesus prayed and also confronted the Pharisees. Jesus prayed and healed people, and he also said to submit to the reigning government. Jesus went off to a secluded place to pray and also flipped tables in the temple. Jesus prayed for us on the cross through surrender and also told the Pharisees the truth when they confronted him. This is why we get to view intercession as both prayer and advocacy work.

In Christian spaces, intercession is often known as praying for people who are suffering, need healing, or are in crisis. It is seen as an emergency-based or intervention-based form of prayer on behalf of others.

Romans 8:34 says, "Who then is the one who condemns? No one. Christ Jesus who died—more than that, who was raised to life—is at the right hand of God and is also interceding for us." And 1 John 2:1 says, "My dear children, I write this to you so that you will not sin. But if anybody does sin, we have an advocate with the Father—Jesus Christ, the Righteous One." Both are examples of intercession. Acts of advocacy and prayer. Therefore, we should see intercession as both prayer and action.

Jesus's disciples didn't know what was to come from following him, but Jesus gave them glimpses of it: "My prayer is not that you take them out of the world but that you protect them from the evil one" (John 17:15). Jesus prays for God to protect the disciples from Satan as they are in the world. This is the very prayer we get to pray not only for our loved ones but also for people on the front lines of war, people on the front lines of social service and justice work, people going through spiritual warfare, and people experiencing suffering. A prayer of protection for what someone is experiencing or will experience is a prayer of intercession that also can be a prayer for justice. Praying for our Black brothers and sisters, that they may not grow weary and dismayed by seeing people of their same skin tone being beaten and killed in the streets by cops, while also praying for the repentance and rebuke of a system that oppresses Black and Brown bodies. Praying for our trafficked brothers and sisters, that they will not lose hope in the idea that they can be free one day, while also praying for the repentance and rebuke of a culture that profits from sex and the use and abuse of bodies. Praying for our church-wounded brothers and sisters, that they will cling to their love for Jesus and not grow bitter because of the brokenness they experienced, while also praying for the repentance and rebuke of churches that protect abusers and congregants who passively do nothing. Prayers for now, for what is to come, and for what should be.

Some people quote the following verse from 2 Chronicles to speak about other people, but it's a passage *about* and *to* all of us. Second Chronicles 7:14 says, "If my people, who are called by my name, will humble themselves and pray and seek my face and turn from their wicked ways, then I will hear from heaven, and I will forgive their sin and will heal their land." This is a message to the Body of Christ. We are his people—the people who bear his name. This is God's call to intercession and repentance. God is saying we must repent and intercede for one another because we need God's forgiveness and healing. Sometimes justice work is repentance.

Intercession can take the form of advocacy through marching, peacefully protesting, donating, volunteering, listening to marginalized voices, calling local elected officials, fighting for our neighbors, and signing petitions. Intercession as advocacy can be done in big and small ways every day of life, but the point is that we can do something. Often we spend so much time thinking about what we can't do that we end up not doing anything at all. That's the enemy's plan. We get to respond by rebuking him and boldly walking in the way of the radical as intercessors.

Being the Hands and Feet of Jesus

Did you know the phrase "being the hands and feet of Jesus" isn't in the Bible? I learned this a few years ago and was so disappointed because it's such a beautiful saying. But it's absolutely Christianese (something that Christians say or a popular saying among Christians). Having said that, I want you to know that the Bible does give us examples of love in action and that when we use this phrase, we are talking about justice work.

What did Jesus's hands and feet do?

They were nailed for our salvation and freedom.
They healed and held people.
They walked alongside people and went from city to city to show people how much God loved them.

When we think about what it means to be Jesus's hands and feet, we should consider how Jesus used his hands and feet. Matthew 20:28 says, "The Son of Man did not come to be served, but to serve, and to give his life as a ransom for many." This is it. He served others.

It's essential we understand that the serving shouldn't be based on our comfort. I know we know this—but do we really? We also need to understand that we may not be able to help all people and show up in every injustice, but we can do something somewhere. We can do things in our everyday lives and local communities to serve the marginalized, overlooked, and least of these, as Jesus describes in Matthew 25:

> "For I was hungry and you gave me something to eat, I was thirsty and you gave me something to drink, I was a stranger and you invited me in, I needed clothes and you clothed me, I was sick and you looked after me, I was in prison and you came to visit me."
>
> Then the righteous will answer him, "Lord, when did we see you hungry and feed you, or thirsty and give you something to drink? When did we see you a stranger and invite you in, or need clothes and clothe you? When did we see you sick or in prison and visit you?"
>
> The King will reply, "Truly I tell you, whatever you did for one of the least of these brothers and sisters of mine, you did for me." (vv. 35–40)

Being Jesus's hands and feet means we give our time, presence, love, compassion, resources, privileges, access, gifts, and energy to radically respond to those who are in need while also responding to the systems that prevent people from accessing the things they need.

Living Out the Fruit of the Spirit

Injustice is often the result of our flesh. Have you ever thought of that? Galatians 5:19–21 says, "The acts of the flesh are obvious:

sexual immorality, impurity and debauchery; idolatry and witchcraft; hatred, discord, jealousy, fits of rage, selfish ambition, dissensions, factions and envy; drunkenness, orgies, and the like."

We won't get into each one, but think about sexual immorality, which is often connected to sex before marriage or adultery. But isn't sexual immorality also sex trafficking and sexual assault? Think about hatred. Is that not the root of racism and any -ism or phobia? Think about outbursts of anger. Aren't they what cause police officers to shoot a Black body over and over again or place their knee on someone's neck? Isn't drunkenness sometimes the cause of nonconsensual sex or car accidents that lead to death? Don't factions create division among communities and people that results in classism, entrenched poverty, and few resources for educational spaces in low-income communities? Doesn't dissension lead to disrespect, dehumanization, and dishonor within the Body of Christ that are representations of injustice?

The flesh is the driving force for injustice in our world. But there's good news in the next few verses in Galatians 5:22–23: "But the fruit of the Spirit is love, joy, peace, forbearance, kindness, goodness, faithfulness, gentleness and self-control. Against such things there is no law."

If you're wondering what fighting injustice looks like, it's living out this fruit by the power of the Holy Spirit within us. This can be seen in our homes, neighborhoods, churches, workplaces, cities, and countries. If every Christian lived out the fruit of the Spirit daily and consistently, so much would change.

Dignifying All Human Beings

We all hold biases, and if not reflected on well, they will result in discrimination, othering, racism, ableism, sexism, classism, belittling, and marginalization. Which is why we should see people as Jesus does, as image bearers. Seeing and treating people with that framework is the work of justice.

Galatians 3:28 says, "There is neither Jew nor Greek, neither slave nor free, nor is there male and female, for you are all one in Christ Jesus." What this doesn't mean is that people can say, "I don't see color," because that's not dignifying. We all have colors and genders and cultures; this was on purpose and given by God. But when we acknowledge that in the kingdom there is neither Jew nor Greek, neither male nor female, we are acknowledging that there is no partiality, no prioritizing some people over others, and no putting people in boxes based on their identity.

Practically, this looks like paying attention to those who have historically not been dignified. The best way to do this is to listen to and learn from these people. You're doing that by reading this book. You do that when you listen to a podcast or a sermon by a person who doesn't look and sound like you. You do that when your friend group reflects the diversity of heaven. You do that when you purposefully live a life that is not homogenous. You choose to live this way not so you can say you are diverse. You do it because Christianity is not a White, rich, or male religion. It is a "Jesus is for all people" faith. This means our stages, spaces, and sanctuaries should look and sound like heaven.

When the Body of Christ is safe, people feel protected, seen, dignified, and welcomed. In the last section of this book, this is what we'll be focusing on: becoming safe people who don't just observe injustice but respond to it. People who choose the way of the radical.

RADICAL THOUGHTS

> Thinking about injustice is not justice work.

> There are simple, everyday things we can do in our homes to live justly, such as recycling, treating our neighbors with dignity, and honoring those we live with.

> Justice doesn't have to be a grandiose step of action. It can be dismantling -isms and phobias in our everyday actions and words.

> Prayer has the power to change things. If we believed this, we could actually change things.

> Justice includes racial things, but it's not always about race. Injustice is found in many areas of life pertaining to socioeconomic status, gender, sexuality, disability, immigration status, experience, and so on.

REFLECTIVE QUESTIONS

> In what ways do you live justly?

> How does your church teach about justice? What does your church do in the area of justice work?

> Why do you think Jesus had a heart for justice?

> What have you been taught about justice in your church, upbringing, community, and culture? Is it biblical?

> How can you become more of a safe person for others?

RESTORATIVE MEDITATION

INHALE: God of justice,
EXHALE: teach us to be like you—a responder to injustice.

INHALE: May the sufferings of this world
EXHALE: be seen and responded to by the Body of Christ.

INHALE: Jesus, take us out of our comfort zones
EXHALE: so we can be a safe and radical presence in this unjust world.

REMAIN IN SCRIPTURE

- o Exodus 3:1–10
- o 2 Chronicles 7:14
- o Isaiah 9:6
- o Matthew 20:28
- o Matthew 25:35–46
- o John 14:27
- o John 17:15
- o Romans 8:34
- o 2 Corinthians 13:11
- o Galatians 3:28
- o Galatians 5:19–23
- o Ephesians 2:14
- o 2 Thessalonians 3:16
- o 1 John 2:1

10

"Go and Do Likewise"

> Christ has no body on earth but yours. Yours are the eyes with which he looks compassionately on this world. Yours are the feet with which he walks to do good. Yours are the hands with which he blesses all the world. Christ has no body now on earth but yours!
>
> —St. Teresa of Ávila[1]

> He answered, "Love the Lord your God with all your heart and with all your soul and with all your strength and with all your mind"; and, "Love your neighbor as yourself."
>
> —Luke 10:27

I have never belonged anywhere. I feel that all of us at some point can relate to that statement. This has been a lifelong narrative for me. The idea of belonging has been far from me and foreign to me. I am a Spanish-speaking Black woman who has struggled to belong to the Black American community because of my language and cultural background. I am a curly-Afro, brown-skinned Latina who has struggled to belong to the Latino community because of my skin tone, hair, and lived experience as a Black woman. I am a daughter of immigrants whose great-grandparents did not live here and whose parents did not buy a home in the 1960s when homes were $1 and that is now my inheritance. I am a daughter of a man who was a superintendent and entrepreneur, which meant we moved a lot and I went to six different schools from pre-K to twelfth grade. I did not find community or stability anywhere—ergo, I did not belong anywhere. I lived in the Dominican Republic as a kid, which is where my family is from, and while there, I did not belong because my Spanish sounded "funny" to people. I still don't belong because I live in the United States and to Dominicans I am a "gringa" and "not really Dominican." I live in the world of Bible teachers and ministry leaders, and although I am pursuing a seminary degree, I don't look like most people who are Bible teachers and Christian leaders in the United States. I'm not conservative, and I'm not liberal. I'm not fully complementarian or egalitarian. I don't belong to a denomination. I'm not Democrat or Republican.

I'm telling you, I don't belong anywhere.

When I was told that I could belong to the Body of Christ by believing in Jesus, you can imagine my shock but also my confusion. Because I haven't belonged anywhere, I didn't know how to belong to the Body of Christ, and neither did the Christians around me. So they taught me how to be the Body in the way they thought we should be, based on what other churches and structures were doing and saying Christianity was.

"You belong before you believe." Some think this is a welcoming statement, but we shouldn't have to tell them they belong before they believe. They should see that, to us and to God, they matter and hold value before they believe. So many people within the church don't feel they belong even after they believe, and that's often because of how they are treated, talked to, and seen. We need to treat others like they belong because of dignity and love.

Another common slogan in many contemporary churches is "Come as you are." You've probably heard it, seen it on a church website, or said it yourself. But what happens when the church begins to lie?

In this section of the book, we are looking at what it means to be a safe place—yes, at a Sunday service but also as a collective Body of people in our everyday living. The phrase "Come as you are" suggests that a place is safe, but words hold no value when people have experiences that contradict the invitation.

We can't say "Come as you are" to people who are disabled and in a wheelchair if our churches don't have ramps or proper access to the facility. Some churches have ushers who lead people in wheelchairs to a place they can be during the service, but dark sanctuaries and flashing lights don't help their experience. Jennifer Ji-Hye Ko, a theologian, advocate, speaker, and wheelchair user, said this to me in a conversation: "Navigating in churches is already difficult for wheelchair users because if the building was built before 1991 it was most likely designed to deliberately exclude people with disabilities. Additionally, if the lights are dim, it's more difficult to navigate. Most wheelchairs have black wheels and structure. This makes running into pews, chairs, people, etc. a greater risk when the lights are dim." If a church is dim or not wheelchair accessible, she can't come as she is.

We can't say "Come as you are" to people who have been historically marginalized and live in a community where they don't belong to the dominant cultural group. If a Black person walks into your church, located in a Black community, and doesn't see a Black pastor or hear a gospel song during the service, they can't really come as they are because who they are hasn't been taken into consideration. This is a disconnect that often happens with church plants. If church planters seek to establish a church in a neighborhood that they know nothing about and made up of people from a culture they have no interest in learning about, then their actual goal is to make the church look like themselves instead of making the church reflect the community.

We can't say "Come as you are" to people who are living in poverty and can't get to a Sunday service because they don't have money for gas or public transportation.

We can't say "Come as you are" to immigrants who are overworked at their jobs because of their citizenship status and don't have Sundays off.

We can't say "Come as you are" to single mothers or fathers who want to come to church but whose kids aren't allowed in the service because they are considered a distraction.

We can't say "Come as you are" to people who are epileptic or neurodivergent and have sensory issues with flashing lights when we aren't willing to let go of the Broadway show lights.

We can't say "Come as you are" to people who are same-sex attracted and are committed to living a holy and communal life with other Christians when we either ignore their sexual orientation or highlight it as something that needs to be prayed away.

We can't say "Come as you are" to people who cannot get out of bed because of their mental health when we don't create opportunities for them to be a part of the church by going to where they are.

"Come as you are" is a false invitation unless we include Christ. It is Christ who convicts, teaches, and leads us to be compassionate people. It is Christ who came to where we are and brought us back home. He says not "Come as you are" but rather "I'm here where you are, and you have a place in my house." That is safety. To know you have somewhere to go and someone to belong to. To know you're protected and kept. To know you are indeed not alone. That is a dignified life. It means you have people who are willing to meet you where you, as you are, with what you need.

If we want to be a Body that is known for justice and just living, then we must consider every image bearer. If we have justice ministries and outreach programs in our churches but are not considering the people coming on Sundays or not able to come on Sundays, then we have missed the mark. We have put on the mask of justice without living it out. I was a social worker for many years and served human trafficking survivors and refugees. Imagine if I treated all those people with dignity and considered their needs and desired growth but went home and treated my husband like I didn't need to listen to him or treated my son a certain way because he's a child. I would need to repent. If this is how we are acting in the church, then our next step is to repent. Then from there, we need to change.

Showing Mercy like Jesus

"Actions speak louder than words" is not just a saying but an invitation to live in integrity. For Christians, it's an invitation to obedience. If we say we love God, then we must love people. If we say we follow Jesus, then we must follow his way of being. If we say we have the Holy Spirit within us, then we must display the fruit of the Spirit.

The Israelites did not get along with a certain group of people, and they mistreated them and discriminated against them. Those people were Samaritans, image bearers who believed in the same God Israel did. Israel claimed to love God but disregarded people who were not like them. It was a "welcome to church but we hate the people across the street" way of living, just as we have all done at some point. I think we have it all wrong. I know we do. We see repeatedly in the Bible a God who advocates for the othered, marginalized, overlooked, dehumanized, oppressed, and forgotten. Examples are found in both the Old Testament and the New Testament.

Let's look at a chapter in biblical history. In 721 BC, Israel was divided in two: the Northern Kingdom of Israel and the Southern Kingdom of Judah. Each kingdom had its own king ruling over its own land. Then Israel was taken over by the Assyrians, and the Israelites were led off as captives. But some stayed in the land and intermarried with non-Israelites. Their children, half-Jewish, half-Gentile, became known as Samaritans. Later on in Israel's story, after the destruction of the temple in 586 BC by the Babylonians, the Samaritans opposed the rebuilding efforts led by Nehemiah. This created deep enmity between Jews and Samaritans.

This historical background helps us understand why Jesus makes a point to note when he's talking about a Samaritan. Plenty of stories in the Bible don't mention someone's ethnicity, race, or gender, but in the case of Samaritans, we almost always know. Why? They are one of the groups Israel mistreated the most and thought the least of.

Let's look at a few Scripture passages where Samaritans are mentioned, as they show Jesus's intention toward these people, despite how other Jewish people saw and treated them. Let's start with the woman at the well: "The Samaritan woman said to him, 'You are a Jew and I am a Samaritan woman. How can you ask me for a drink?' (For Jews do not associate with Samaritans.)" (John 4:9). Note that the woman at the well is alluding to the long-standing divides between Israelites and Samaritans. She is shocked or confused as to why Jesus would talk to her.

This woman has gone to the well in the middle of the day at its hottest point because she knows no one will be there. She goes at that time not to avoid a long line but because she knows if she went at another time, she would be ridiculed, judged, and maybe even mistreated. Yet what she finds there is a safe place. Jesus shows love and wants her to experience real freedom. He meets her in a place where she normally feels shame and offers her salvation. He is a safe place.

Then at the beginning of Acts, after Jesus has died and been resurrected, he is leaving instructions for his disciples. He says, "But you will receive power when the Holy Spirit comes on you; and you will be my witnesses in Jerusalem, and in all Judea and Samaria, and to the ends of the earth" (1:8).

Jerusalem was in Judea, and there were seven other regions in that area, including Galilee, Phoenicia, and Perea, but Jesus mentions Samaria. In his final words to his disciples, he reminds them that he came even for those the Jews have issues with and try to ignore. He reminds them that the good news is for all people, including the ones they probably don't want to tell the good news to. He reminds them that salvation is for all people, including the people they have historically mistreated. Thankfully, some of those disciples listen. In Acts 8:4–6, we read this: "Those who had been scattered preached the word wherever they went. Philip went down to a city in Samaria and proclaimed the Messiah there. When the crowds heard Philip and saw the signs he performed, they all paid close attention to what he said."

Perhaps the most well-known passage that mentions a Samaritan is found in the Gospel of Luke. It's the parable of the good Samaritan.

An expert in the law asks Jesus a question he already knows the answer to: "Teacher, . . . what must I do to inherit eternal life?" (Luke 10:25). And Jesus responds.

> "What is written in the Law?" he replied. "How do you read it?"
>
> He answered, "'Love the Lord your God with all your heart and with all your soul and with all your strength and with all your mind'; and, 'Love your neighbor as yourself.'"
>
> "You have answered correctly," Jesus replied. "Do this and you will live."
>
> But he wanted to justify himself, so he asked Jesus, "And who is my neighbor?" (vv. 26–29)

Jesus then goes on to tell the story of the good Samaritan.

> A man was going down from Jerusalem to Jericho, when he was attacked by robbers. They stripped him of his clothes, beat him and went away, leaving him half dead. A priest happened to be going down the same road, and when he saw the man, he passed by on the other side. So too, a Levite, when he came to the place and saw him, passed by on the other side. But a Samaritan, as he traveled, came where the man was; and when he saw him, he took pity on him. He went to him and bandaged his wounds, pouring on oil and wine. Then he put the man on his own don-

> key, brought him to an inn and took care of him. The next day he took out two denarii and gave them to the innkeeper. "Look after him," he said, "and when I return, I will reimburse you for any extra expense you may have." (Luke 10:30–35)

Then Jesus asks a question different from the one he was originally asked. The expert in the law asked, "Who is my neighbor?" but Jesus asks, "Which of these three do you think was a neighbor to the man who fell into the hands of robbers?" (Luke 10:36). Jesus does not just point out who our neighbors are—which was the original question of the teacher of the law—he explains what it means to be neighborly. It is one thing to know that all people in the world are image bearers who are deeply loved by God. It is another thing altogether to love people in the world as image bearers who are deeply loved by God. Knowing God loves people is beautiful, but it doesn't require anything of us. Loving the very people God loves requires us to be a neighbor.

After Jesus asks the question, the expert in the law says, "The one who had mercy on him." Jesus tells him, "Go and do likewise" (Luke 10:37). Mercy in this verse is translated from the Greek word *eleos*, which means "kindness or good will toward the miserable and the afflicted, joined with a desire to help them."[2] This is the vision God has for us. To not just be observers like the Levite and the priest. To not just be observers of tragedy, trauma, and terrible news. To be like the Samaritan who stopped to help. There's a Spanish proverb that says, *Ojos que no ven, corazón que no siente*—if I don't see it, then I don't need to feel anything about it. Perhaps that's what the Levite and the priest who passed by were thinking. But not the Samaritan—he chose to see this man.

He could have just had a heart to be kind and good toward those who are afflicted, but *eleos* tells us that the Samaritan was more than just kind and good. He turned his kindness and goodness into fuel to help the broken and beaten person on the road. Who was this person? We don't know his story, race, age, socioeconomic status, or family status. Why? Because none of those things matter in the eyes of a righteous God. He sees an image bearer worthy of dignity every time. This is our call too. To go and do the same as the Samaritan and to go and do the same as God himself—the one who has given us *eleos* all our lives, not because we are good or kind but because he loves us.

In the next chapter, we'll talk about some tangible ways to be a neighbor by seeing our neighbor, but I'll close with this story.

In 1969, Black citizens of the United States were not allowed to swim in pools that were designated Whites only. Fred Rogers, also known as Mr. Rogers, invited a Black police officer to join him on an episode of his television show. He filled up a small pool and invited the officer to dip his feet into the pool to cool down. Mr. Rogers also put his feet in the water. Many Christians simply talk about being a neighbor. But Mr. Rogers chose the radical way of being like Jesus by responding to Jesus's call to "go and do likewise." He created a safe place for the Black officer not just to cool down but to be seen as a person. He could have just talked about this issue on his show, but instead he chose to be about it. He didn't save the Black man, and he wasn't trying to. He was just trying to show others that this Black man is worthy of dignity. Maybe, just maybe, that's what the good Samaritan was trying to do. While most people in the 1960s were living divided like the Jews and Samaritans, Mr. Rogers chose to live like his Savior and invite a man to a well, and that made all the difference.

RADICAL THOUGHTS

> "Come as you are" is an empty phrase if not accompanied by action and a culture that promotes safety.

> Performative justice does harm just like injustice does.

> Justice is not a trend.

> Being committed to being a safe person is one of the most Christlike things we can do.

> Living justly should be a part of how we create structures and culture in our churches.

REFLECTIVE QUESTIONS

> What's the last justice-oriented action you took?

> How do you intentionally consider other people who are overlooked and forgotten?

> Have you taken the time to notice how your church treats "other" people and if there's space for all people to be welcome there?

> What is something new you've learned about the Samaritans or the conflict between Israel and Samaria that you want to reflect more on?

RESTORATIVE MEDITATION

INHALE: God of Israel,
EXHALE: thank you for being the God of all people.

INHALE: Holy Spirit, ignite a fire in us to go and do the same.
EXHALE: May the mercy you give us move us to do just that.

REMAIN IN SCRIPTURE

o Nehemiah 6
o Luke 10:25–37
o John 4:9
o Acts 1:8
o Acts 8:4–6

11

Beloved before Anything

> To be free is not merely to cast off one's chains, but to live in a way that respects and enhances the freedom of others.
>
> —Nelson Mandela[1]

> We demolish arguments and every pretension that sets itself up against the knowledge of God, and we take captive every thought to make it obedient to Christ.
>
> —2 Corinthians 10:4–5 CSB

I've been called a heretic by a stranger who decided they didn't want to consider my humanity first. I've been called the N-word by someone who decided I had no worth or dignity. I've been called offended by someone who was supposed to be my spiritual leader instead of that person acknowledging the harm they caused me. I have been called many things. The one name I have held to is *beloved.*

> See what kind of love the Father has given to us, that we should be called children of God; and so we are. The reason why the world does not know us is that it did not know him. Beloved, we are God's children now, and what we will be has not yet appeared; but we know that when he appears we shall be like him, because we shall see him as he is. (1 John 3:1–2 ESV)

As Christians, we aren't just image bearers, although that holds great value. We are also God's children. We are also beloved. Because we are those things, in many ways we are unseen by the world, so we can stop striving to live up to the world's standards. We don't need to prove the majesty and power of God to anyone. Most see and experience God through the testimonies and lives of others. If we live justly and humbly, people will surely see the Spirit of the living God within us. But while we do that, we need to know and understand that we won't always be called things that are pleasant, dignifying, or true. Just as Jesus wasn't. But what is true is that we are image bearers, beloved, and children of God. Although being children of God is reserved for those who follow Jesus, to be a beloved image bearer worthy of dignity is something God says we all have access to.

In the previous chapter, we looked at Luke's version of the greatest commandment. In Matthew 22:37–39, Jesus says, "'Love the Lord your God with all your heart and with all your soul and with all your mind.' This is the first and greatest commandment. And the second is like it: 'Love your neighbor as yourself.'" Jesus wasn't making up new ideas, concepts, or commandments. He was reiterating Deuteronomy 6:5 and Leviticus 19:18. Because Jesus is God, he affirms what God has already said.

If we consider who we are in Christ, which is beloved, then perhaps we can see that the invitation to love our neighbor as ourselves is an invitation to love others as beloved human beings. There are many ways to do this. One way is to be committed to the cause of Christ by helping to restore what humanity has broken. Brokenness has resulted in sexism, racism, ageism, ableism, homophobia, abuse, oppression, and any other -ism, phobia, or dehumanization we can think of that opposes the narrative that people are indeed beloved.

Loving our neighbor means we see our neighbor as beloved and we live in a way that exemplifies advocacy, mutuality, and honor for every image bearer, not just other Christians. In many ways, this is the Great Commission (Matt. 28:18–20)—the invitation to go to all people and tell them that God calls them beloved, to love them enough to fight for them and their spiritual, physical, emotional, financial, educational, ancestral, and religious freedom.

How do we do this? We advocate.

Advocacy is often seen as applying only to people working in social services, activism, justice, or law work. But imagine if God restricted advocacy to only people in those career paths? If we are like God, as 1 John 3:1–2 tells us, then we are advocates like he is.

Here's the truth: how people perceive Christianity is often how they perceive Christ, and how they perceive Christ affects how they perceive themselves. When they perceive themselves as the beloved of Christ, they will live in a way that is good for the world and glorifies God. It's a circle of sorts, and that circle starts with us. So living out the Great Commission starts with our day-to-day thoughts, actions, and words.

This chapter examines three groups of people who are our beloved neighbors whom we get to love, see, and fight for.

Our Nearest Neighbor

It seems that we have forgotten that those right in front of us are our neighbors. Our siblings, spouses, kids, and parents are our neighbors because a neighbor is anyone who isn't us. When we serve in our home and show those within it that they hold value, regardless of what they believe and what decisions they've made, we are being like Jesus and loving our neighbor.

Jesus and the disciples weren't related by blood, but to one another they were family. They did everything together for three years. Jesus considered the disciples his brothers, and right before he was about to be killed, he took a moment to remind them how seen they were: "So he got up from the meal, took off his outer clothing, and wrapped a towel around his waist. After that, he poured water into a basin and began to wash his disciples' feet, drying them with the towel that was wrapped around him" (John 13:4–5).

The God of the universe washed the disciples' dirty feet. Because he loved them. He saw them. He understood that they had value, and not because of anything they'd done but simply because he decided it was so. There were disciples older than him and younger than him. There were faithful disciples and deceptive ones. There were consistent ones and inconsistent ones. They were sinners and saints. Yet none of those identities qualified them or disqualified them for Jesus to show them one last time that he saw them as beloved.

Within many of our homes there is pain and trauma. There is suffering and fighting. There is disagreement and disrespect. Jesus experienced all of that with his disciples. Yet he did not let that stop him from expressing his love. Boundaries are important and healthy, but what is also true is that every person is our neighbor, including the people in our homes and families.

Our "Different from Us" Neighbor

People right now are living a completely different life from yours. This is because they are choosing to or because their identity forces them to live a certain way because of how society is structured. Women aren't choosing to be paid less than men. They aren't choosing to live a life that is financially unstable. Asian people aren't choosing to be targeted by racists. They aren't choosing to live in fear and grief. People in wheelchairs aren't choosing to be denied access to buildings or public transportation. They literally cannot get around if where they live isn't built for their lived experience.

We have become so jaded by the news, a misunderstanding of social justice and liberation movements, and bad biblical teaching that we miss compassion altogether. We miss believing people. We miss the Truth for other truths that are based on what we think and see. But the world didn't begin with our thoughts and perspectives but with Christ and every true word spoken by his mouth. So if our thoughts do not align with the way of the radical, Scripture has a response to that: "We demolish arguments and every pretension that sets itself up against the knowledge of God, and we take captive every thought to make it obedient to Christ" (2 Cor. 10:4–5).

We get to go to Jesus with every thought that is shaped by our upbringings, communities, traditions, teachings, and cultures that doesn't align with God and his Word. We submit those thoughts to Jesus, and in exchange he gives us the truth and wisdom.

The book of Numbers is a census of sorts. It includes numbers, history, and genealogy. In chapter 27 is a story in which Moses shows us how to see our "different" neighbor:

> So Moses brought their case before the LORD, and the LORD said to him, "What Zelophehad's daughters are saying is right. You must certainly give them property as an inheritance among their father's relatives and give their father's inheritance to them.
>
> "Say to the Israelites, 'If a man dies and leaves no son, give his inheritance to his daughter. If he has no daughter, give his inheritance to his brothers. If he has no brothers, give his inheritance to his father's brothers. If his father had no brothers, give his inheritance to the nearest relative in his clan, that he may possess it. This is to have the force of law for the Israelites, as the LORD commanded Moses.'" (Num. 27:5–11)

Moses didn't know what it was like to be a woman or to be denied an inheritance. The daughters of Zelophehad had a different lived experience, and Moses could have ignored them because he couldn't relate to or understand their circumstance. Instead, he brought their situation to God, and God instructed him on how to address it. Because of the time Moses was living in, he likely had some thoughts about the situation as a man and leader, but he brought those thoughts to God, and God exchanged Moses's limited perspective for truth.

Racism, sexism, homophobia, classism, and ableism all happen because we fail to see the person as an image bearer and we can't relate to or understand their circumstance. But just because we can't relate to people doesn't mean we should treat them poorly. Instead, we should treat them like Jesus does—with unconditional love. He doesn't love me because I'm a woman or because of my age or education. He loves those things about me, but that's not why he loves me. If he loved us for certain things, then he might also *not* love us for certain other things, but that's never the case.

Someone in my life identifies as "they." I cannot relate and don't fully understand, but I choose to love this person and show them the Christ I follow by the way I live and the way I treat others. Not directly confronting their situation doesn't mean I affirm it. It means I see the dignity in them before I try to teach them anything. Dignifying someone and disagreeing with them is not an oxymoron. Also, if they aren't following Jesus, shouldn't I be evangelizing them before inviting them to any other path or restoration? Too often we expect people to change before we even introduce them to Christ.

When an injustice happens, one side will say, "That person was so nice—they didn't deserve that injustice," and the other side will say, "They were a criminal and deserved that." Neither perspective is good because they both dismiss the belovedness of someone by placing value on them based on what they did or didn't do. That's simply not how God sees people. Instead, we should respond like Moses did: check our opinions at the door and go to God and his Word for guidance and answers.

Our "In Tangible Need" Neighbor

Let's look again at the parable of the good Samaritan: "But a Samaritan, as he traveled, came where the man was; and when he saw him, he took pity on him. He went to him and bandaged his wounds, pouring on oil and wine. Then he put the man on his own donkey, brought him to an inn and took care of him. The next day he took out two denarii and gave them to the innkeeper. 'Look after him,' he said, 'and when I return, I will reimburse you for any extra expense you may have'" (Luke 10:33–35). Verse 33 contains something we don't want to miss: the Samaritan saw the man and had compassion on him. The Greek word for "compassion" in this verse is *splanchnizomai*, and it means "to be moved in the inward parts."[2] The definition refers to bowel movements, but I wonder if it could also refer to the Spirit moving within us. Much of what shows up in our bodies physically is a manifestation of emotions, our mental state, and memories. I would add that spiritual manifestations show up in our bodies too because the Holy Spirit lives in our minds and hearts. The one who leads us to conviction can lead us to compassion too.

The Samaritan didn't just serve the man; he saw him. He humbled himself to relate to him. My son is very friendly and energetic and loves to play, but when I get on his level and sit on the ground with him, he goes all out and gets so excited. Is it always comfortable for me? No, but I'm choosing to serve him beyond my comfort level. Seeing our neighbor has so much to do with the position we are willing to put ourselves in. Isn't that what Christ did? Lowered himself from heaven to be with us? Lowered himself from King to be killed on a cross? The marginalized need us to humble ourselves enough for us to see them with dignity but also to acknowledge how much there is to learn from them.

There are people living on your block or in your neighborhood you don't know or don't see. There are also people you've met. You know their names and testimonies. Aren't the ones you don't see or know worthy of the same dignity you show the neighbors you do know?

Seeing is about not just what you see with your eyes but also what you think about people, whether near or far, personal or impersonal, relatable or distant. What do you think of the image bearer who is your neighbor? The nearby one, the different one, and the one in need. The way of the radical is about seeing all people. Remembering that they are beloved before anything else and knowing that is reason enough to be an advocate for them and a safe place for them to land and to be loved.

RADICAL THOUGHTS

> Serve those around you first.

> Not all help is help. Don't be a savior. Ask what others need.

> Respect and love don't mean agreement or affirmation. They show that you see the dignity in an image bearer. Respect and love others.

> We don't need proximity to people to be a neighbor. We need proximity to Scripture. Be in the Word.

> Seeing others is listening to others.

> Die to yourself and to the ideologies you were taught that aren't God glorifying. Unlearn and deconstruct.

> Always ask yourself, "What would be the most effective way to serve this person that would also glorify God and honor them?"

> Always remember your testimony. Remember the grace you needed and still need—and extend the same to others.

REFLECTIVE QUESTIONS

> Could your family and friends recall the last time you served them lovingly and intentionally?

> What thoughts have you had about a person you know or don't know that were not dignifying based on their race, gender, disability, lived experience, and so on?

> Is there anything God is inviting you to repent of based on the topic of this chapter?

> Do you feel like evangelism and justice are separate things? If so, why?

> Where has your view of justice or evangelism come from, and is it biblically accurate?

> Do you belong to a marginalized group? What has been your experience of feeling beloved by God despite the world not thinking this of you?

> How can you begin or continue to see your neighbor and show them how beloved they are?

> Are the majority of authors you read, hosts of podcasts you listen to, preachers of sermons you learn from, people you interact with, and people who mentor or minister to you people of the same gender, race, ethnicity, ability, gifts, denomination, age, relationship status, and so on as you? If so, how can you consider changing this?

RESTORATIVE MEDITATION

INHALE: "Sin separated, the breach was far too wide, but from the far side of the chasm, You held me in your sight."[3]

EXHALE: God is El Roi—the God who sees me does the same for others because I am the neighbor my neighbors need.

REMAIN IN SCRIPTURE

- o Genesis 1:26–27
- o Numbers 27:5–11
- o Micah 6:8
- o Matthew 22:37–39
- o Matthew 25:31–46
- o Matthew 28:18–20
- o Luke 10:33–35
- o John 3:16–17
- o John 13:4–5
- o Romans 5:6–8
- o 1 Corinthians 3:16
- o 2 Corinthians 2:4–5
- o Galatians 3:28
- o 1 John 3:1–2
- o 1 John 3:17

12

Being Sanctuaries

With thanksgiving, I'll be a living sanctuary for you.

—Randy Scruggs and John Thompson,
"Lord, Prepare Me to Be a Sanctuary"[1]

Jesus replied, "Anyone who loves me will obey my teaching. My Father will love them, and we will come to them and make our home with them."

—John 14:23

The word *sanctuary* means a place of consecration, refuge, and safety.[2] It describes a place that is safe from danger, oppression, abuse, and suffering. Some places in the United States are called "sanctuary cities," where undocumented immigrants are protected from deportation or prosecution through municipal laws.

As Christians, we are a people, but we are also a place. We are a temple that the Holy Spirit calls home, and we can and should be a place that people call sacred, soft, and safe. We should be known as a place where people can feel safe from danger, abuse, dehumanization, and suffering—on Sundays at a building but also Monday through Saturday wherever we are, because that is what the church is: a living Body actively present in the world all days of the week, not just on Sunday.

We can put up signs outside our churches that say "Welcome home" or invite people into our lives, but our actions are what will most communicate welcome.

The thing about being sanctuaries is that we must be aware that people are looking for us. People are looking to feel safe, seen, and surrounded wherever they are. They are looking for places and people who exude goodness, gentleness, peace, love, joy, faithfulness, self-control, kindness, and forbearance. Both Christians and non-Christians are looking for this fruit, and that's one of the most important things to not miss in being a sanctuary. When we choose to be a sanctuary, we are a people and a place that are safe for all people, like Jesus was and is.

The Pharisees and those deemed unclean went to Jesus.
The children and the demon possessed went to Jesus.
The Jews and the Gentiles went to Jesus.
The woman with the issue of blood and Zacchaeus went to Jesus.

Jesus lived, talked, and walked like a sanctuary. This doesn't mean Jesus wasn't direct and didn't confront sin. This doesn't mean Jesus treated some people better than others. This doesn't mean Jesus expected all those around him to immediately act like him. Instead, he simply was a living sanctuary for all of them, and that changed their lives forever. Jesus changes everything, and that includes us. We must be willing to change our minds, repent, shift, return, and live out the gospel like we know it's true.

Here's the truth: this book isn't communicating something new. That's why it's not called *Becoming a Sanctuary*. Becoming something means we were not originally that thing. But from the beginning, God created us to be his Body. And we are living out that plan right now in real time. He created us to be sanctuaries. It's what we were meant to be. Therefore, our response is to *be* in Christ and *be like* Christ, not try to *become* Christ. He alone is God, and we get to be his faithful followers. Living sanctuaries.

What Does the Lord Require?

There's a misconception in the Christian faith that Jesus just wants to be with us and doesn't require anything of us. But we see in the Old Testament and the New Testament examples of the opposite. In the Old Testament, God requires certain structures, lifestyles, and rhythms in order for his people to be holy. In the New Testament, Jesus begins his ministry with a word of repentance (Matt. 4:17) and goes on to tell people to die to themselves (Luke 9:23), take up their cross (Matt. 16:24), receive the Holy Spirit, and so much more. The New Testament even tells us that we can't receive the Holy Spirit unless we repent and follow Jesus (Acts 2:38). The word *requirement* might sound "religious" to some of us, but requirements are a part of our decision to follow Jesus. He requires certain things of us not because we are robots or because he wants us to be in bondage but because he loves us and wants us to be free.

There are things God requires of us if we are to be his sanctuary here on earth and have a relationship with him. A verse in the Bible actually asks the question "What does the LORD require of you?" It's Micah 6:8: "He has told you, O man, what is good; and what does the LORD require of you but to do justice, and to love kindness, and to walk humbly with your God?" (ESV).

We often find the second half of this verse on mugs or T-shirts, but Scripture is whole. The second half of the verse is merely an encouragement if we miss the first half. The first half states two things:

1. God has told us what is good. We don't need to seek to find it. He said it in the beginning of Genesis and continued to do so throughout the Bible.
2. The Lord requires some things of us. Not so we can earn his love, accomplish something for him, or be able to be the ultimate Christians but because he knows that what he requires of us is good both for us and for humanity.

Micah 6:8 communicates a few things God requires of us. To do justice, to love kindness, and to walk humbly with our God.

What does it mean to do justice?

What does it mean to love kindness?

What does it mean to walk humbly with our God?

And why would God require these particular things?

This book is an open door to consider what it looks like to live, act, talk, think, and be like Jesus. This book is not meant to replace your Bible study time but to be an encouragement to live out what you learn from the Bible. To be sanctuaries.

It's meant to show you what might be making you live as the Body of Christ in a way that is passive, observant, or lukewarm.

It's meant to make you reflect and wonder, not feel bad or offended. It's meant to move you closer to Christ and the maturity he's inviting you to. Much of that maturity will come from living justly, loving kindness, and not just walking with God but *humbly* walking with him. It's meant to help you understand that you indeed get to be a sacred, soft, and safe place for people to land.

Both our Christian and non-Christian neighbors are looking for a place that offers more than shiny lights, Twitterable sermons, and surface relationships. They are looking for a place that reflects the Jesus we have come to know and love. They are looking for a place to call home and a people who will see more than their sin and will love them enough to treat them with compassion. A people to call family so they can keep going even when life is at its hardest. A people to call trustworthy so they can share their stories of what they've done and what's been done to them. A people to call the Body of Christ who will both teach and live out sound biblical doctrine. A people and a place that are sacred, soft, and safe.

Do Justice

In chapters 9–11, we talked about what living out justice looks like, but what does that look like in your life personally, in your context? As a woman of color, I'm constantly having to think about justice because I live in a world not made for my dignity. The systems and structures that plague my community, gender, neighborhood, and culture are not things I am privileged to forget about. But even those things are not my motivation for doing justice. We must do justice because the Lord does it, requires it, and loves it.

We can start simple. Do you recycle? That's part of environmental justice and a response to Genesis 1:26. God has given us this earth as a home, and we must steward it. In daily acts of choosing to be a sanctuary, we recognize that we live in a gift that is a sanctuary.

Sometimes we try to be a hero and a savior. But even simple acts of doing justice fulfill this requirement of God. To do justice is to be a contributor to the just work God is already doing.

Love Kindness

Some translations of Micah 6:8 contain the word *mercy*, and others contain the word *kindness*, and although these words are important, I think the biggest requirement here is to love. We can do and say kind or merciful things, but the word *love* is an invitation to examine the heart behind saying or doing the kind or merciful thing. Do we love to be kind to others? Do we love to be merciful toward others? I get that some people are hard to love. But those people also deeply need Jesus, just like anyone else.

Ultimately, this requirement is about loving others, not because they deserve it but because God invites us to love people as he loves them. To extend mercy as he does. In Micah 7:18, we read that God delights in showing mercy. It's not just something he does—he delights in doing so. This is what makes him a sanctuary. We can go to him with all we are, and still he delights in forgiving us and showing us mercy. No matter what we've done and where we've been.

What would it look like if the church did this with the intent of being a sanctuary instead of the sin police? Legalism is ineffective, and passivity doesn't honor God. Those two extremes don't have loving-kindness at their center, but being a sanctuary does.

Walk Humbly with God

What a wild and beautiful invitation it is to walk with God. I see this as a twofold blessing. He requires this because he knows what the path looks like when we don't walk with him (see the story of Eve in the garden when she was not walking with God but talking to the serpent instead) and because he knows the freedom that comes with walking humbly with him. When we walk humbly with God, we see immigrants beyond their citizenship status. When we walk humbly with God, we care about the church enough to be a contributor to her health instead of just an observer of her downfall. When we walk humbly with God, we show up for people and meet them where they are. When we walk humbly with God, we represent him in radically beautiful ways that minister to non-Christians. When we walk humbly with God, we repent instead of suppressing or trying to cover up our sin. When we walk humbly with God, we are being the Body of Christ well. We are choosing to be sanctuaries by walking humbly with the one who was the first sanctuary.

What Do We Do Now?

Notice that of the three things the Lord requires of us, two involve other people. This is another reminder that we are to be sanctuaries because sanctuaries are where people are and want to be. That's why they exist. They are sacred places for people to feel safe. Sanctuaries are where people experience justice, heal from injustice, and are advocated for in the face of injustice.

Sanctuaries are where people experience loving-kindness and mercy, are taught how to extend kindness and mercy, and have kindness and mercy toward themselves. The Body of Christ has a great responsibility, and we can respond to it by walking a different path.

Christian philosopher Esther Lightcap Meek says, "A pilgrimage of knowing can be a journey of course corrections."[3] What happens when you're confronted with the truth? You can either keep walking the path you're on or move in a different direction. Humbly walking with God involves doing the latter.

This chapter ends slightly different from the others. First, I'd like to give you some questions to reflect on. One of the biggest errors we can make in this age of information and technology is to consume lots of great ideas, practices, and wisdom, but then just keep moving like nothing happened. So we are going to end this book the way we began—with an invitation (to reflect on these questions) and a selah (on the following page).

REFLECTIVE QUESTIONS

> As you read this chapter and this book, what came up for you that you're wrestling with?

> How do you see yourself as a contributing member of the Body of Christ?

> Why do all these issues, topics, ideas, and points matter to God?

> Why does all of this matter to you?

> Now that you're fully aware of all of this, what will you do with it?

> What is God inviting you to do next? Is he inviting you to repent, reflect, respond, or something else?

> Will you be a radical and walk in the way of Jesus, unapologetically and uncompromised?

SELAH POSTLUDE

Restorative Radicals

There is a high, holy, humble, and hard call God is opening a door for.

High above what we've assumed to be church.

Holy in its foundational framework and path.

Humble in choosing sanctification and gentleness over success and powerhouses.

Hard, but if done collectively, effective, edifying, and extravagantly beautiful.

I hope, friend, with the sincerest of words, that you will say yes to the way of the radical.

For the glory of God, global goodness, and a grand liberation for your very own soul.

And the church said, "Amen."

Acknowledgments

I love that I get to write this section because one of my love languages is celebrating others, and although I can't get to every person who prayed for and supported me, I will try my best.

I want to give God glory for my mami, Daisy Perreaux. What a living vessel. She not only consistently came to my house to take care of my son while I wrote but also encouraged me and constantly told me how proud she was of me. I am here because of my mother—her sacrifices, intelligence, wisdom, prayers, love, and support.

Can we give a round of applause to my husband, Emanuel Dominguez? For being a consistent encouragement in my life and giving me feedback that keeps me going. For also being with our son and putting him to sleep most nights when I was in our room writing this book. For supporting the entirety of all I'm called to even beyond this book. For teaching me how to be a radical Christian by loving the forgotten and practicing forgiveness like no one else I've seen.

To my *familia*—my brothers, Luis and Eric, and their families, and Tia Grey, her kids, and her kids' kids. I have a very large family (Latina after all), but these people have been the ones who have celebrated me the most. I'm grateful for their support and always lifting me up even in the midst of small accomplishments.

To my community in New York City—thank you for being shoulders to cry on, hearts to hug, and minds to process with. Thank you for grounding me and loving me well. Thank you for showing me what it means to be the Body of Christ.

To my friends all over the world—I love that I've met so many people online who have become real-life friends. You know who you are, and I'm eternally grateful for your support and for cheering me on from afar and up close. I thank you for your prayers, feedback, encouragement, and love.

To my community of writers—I never even thought I belonged to that calling until y'all welcomed me in. Thank you for welcoming me with open arms and affirming my calling.

To the Full Collective tribe—y'all are faithful! Thank you for riding with me since 2018 and believing in the work I do even if the mission has changed over time. Thank you for showing up and supporting me. Thank you for being willing to talk about hard things and trust me with adventures around the world. Thank you for responding to the invitation from God to live a *full* life.

To my beloved friend Ashley Abercrombie—this book wouldn't exist without you. You are a grand slam of a human being, and I'm so grateful for how you welcomed me into your arms when I walked into your home as a stranger that evening in fall 2017. You saw beyond my brokenness and lifted me up. Thank you for being a friend, mentor, pastor, cheerleader, coach, and sister. I will never have enough words to thank you.

To my agent, Rachel—thank you for believing in me beyond numbers and seeing the message and my heart. Thank you for seeing the potential in me and listening to my "out there" book idea. Thank you for believing in it from day one.

To my editor and publishing team—thank you for being on my team before I signed anything. Thank you for believing in my ministry and message before I said yes. Thank you for taking a chance on me and seeing the purpose of this book. I couldn't have asked for a better first-time author experience with all of you. Truly so thankful.

To the church—I love you forever, and I will stick beside you as long as it takes.

Notes

Introduction

1. "Come Again" by Maverick City, written by Chandler Moore, Brandon Lake, Steven Furtick, and Dante Bowe, track 1 on disc 2 of *Old Church Basement* (Elevation Worship and Provident Label Group, 2021).

2. *Oxford English Dictionary*, s.v. "crisis," accessed February 8, 2024, https://www.oed.com/dictionary/crisis_n; see also https://www.google.com/search?hl=en&q=crisis meaning.

Chapter 1 Selah Will Be Our Saving Grace

1. "A Beautiful Chicago Kid," by Common, written by Lonnie Lynn, Paris Jones, Karriem Riggins, Isaiah Sharkey, and Burniss Travis, track 2 on *A Beautiful Revolution Pt. 2* (Loma Vista, 2021).

2. "One of the Most Important Lessons Dr. Maya Angelou Ever Taught Oprah | The Oprah Winfrey Show | OWN," YouTube video, 1:07, posted by OWN on May 19, 2014, https://youtu.be/nJgmaHkcFP8.

Chapter 2 Higher and Holier

1. "The Miseducation of Lauryn Hill," by Lauryn Hill, written by Lauryn Hill and Tejumold Newton, track 14 on *The Miseducation of Lauryn Hill* (Ruffhouse, Columbia, 1998).

2. @robspalace, "All jokes aside. Our letter would be devastating," TikTok, December 27, 2022, https://www.tiktok.com/@robspalace_/video/7182013528507829546.

3. Andrew Root and Blair D. Bertrand, *When Church Stops Working: A Future for Your Congregation beyond More Money, Programs, and Innovation* (Grand Rapids: Brazos, 2023), 9.

Chapter 3 The Roots of Uniformity and the Road toward Unity

1. Gwendolyn Brooks, "Paul Robeson," in *The Essential Gwendolyn Brooks* (New York: Library of America, 2005).

2. Martin Luther King Jr., on *Meet the Press*, NBC, April 17, 1960, available at https://youtu.be/1q881g1L_d8.

3. Mark Charles and Soong-Chan Rah, *Unsettling Truths: The Ongoing, Dehumanizing Legacy of the Doctrine of Discovery* (Downers Grove, IL: InterVarsity, 2019), 15.

4. "Fluorescent and LED Lighting and Autism Spectrum Disorder," Make Great Light, May 14, 2021, https://www.makegreatlight.com/about-us/blog/fluorescent-led-lighting-autism-spectrum-disorder.

5. Addison Waters, "Community Needs Assessment: The Resources and Examples Your Organization Needs," Get Connected, December 13, 2023, https://www.galaxydigital.com/blog/community-needs-assessment.

Chapter 4 Taking Sanctification Seriously

1. Stanley Hauerwas, *A Community of Character: Toward a Constructive Christian Social Ethic* (Notre Dame, IN: University of Notre Dame Press, 1981).

2. *Oxford English Dictionary*, s.v. "sanctification," accessed February 8, 2024, https://www.oed.com/dictionary/sanctification_n; see also https://www.google.com/search?hl=en&q=sanctification meaning.

3. Caitlin Mazur, "40+ Worrisome Workplace Stress Statistics [2023]: Facts, Causes, and Trends," Zippia, February 11, 2023, https://www.zippia.com/advice/workplace-stress-statistics.

4. Cole Arthur Riley, *This Here Flesh: Spirituality, Liberation, and the Stories That Make Us* (New York: Convergent, 2020), 157.

5. *Merriam-Webster*, s.v. "dignity," accessed February 8, 2024, https://www.merriam-webster.com/dictionary/dignity.

6. Emily V. Vogels, Monica Anderson, Margaret Porteus, Chris Baronavski, Sara Atske, Colleen McClain, Brooke Auxier, Andrew Perrin, and Meera Ramshankar, "Americans and 'Cancel Culture': Where Some See Calls for Accountability, Others See Censorship, Punishment," Pew Research, May 19, 2021, https://www.pewresearch.org/internet/2021/05

/19/americans-and-cancel-culture-where-some-see-calls-for-accountability-others-see-censorship-punishment.

Chapter 5 A Call to Collective Suffering, or Practicing Presence

1. Tori Peterson (@torihopepetersen), "I wrote this quote years ago," Instagram, August 31, 2023, https://www.instagram.com/reel/CwnJVSCATrq.

2. "Reply All: The 6.1.14 Issue," *New York Times*, June 13, 2014, https://www.nytimes.com/2014/06/15/magazine/reply-all-the-6-114-issue.html.

Chapter 6 A Place for the Weary, Wounded, and Wandering

1. "You're Not Wrong" by Common Hymnal, written by Gabriella Velez, Bryan Joy, James Paek, and Mark Alan Schoolmeesters, © 2022 Common Hymnal Publishing, G Velez Music, BJOY Musics, Common Hymnal Digital, J Paek Music, Standing Room Only, https://commonhymnal.com/songs/youre-not-wrong.

2. Beth Allison Barr (@bethallisonbarr), "It seems to me that," Threads, February 1, 2024, 8:15 a.m., https://www.threads.net/@bethallisonbarr/post/C2zmHmQLw9h.

Chapter 7 Living in Sighs and Silence

1. Toni Morrison, interview with Elsie B. Washington, "Talk with Toni Morrison," *Essence* (October 1987), quoted in *Conversations with Toni Morrison*, ed. Danille Kathleen Taylor-Guthrie (Jackson: University Press of Mississippi, 1994), 237.

Chapter 8 Souls over Sides and Stances

1. Suzy Kassem, *Rise Up and Salute the Sun: The Writings of Suzy Kassem*, ed. Ryan Grim (Boston: Awakened Press, 2011).

2. Jack Jenkins, "The Insurrectionists' Senate Floor Prayer Highlights a Curious Trumpian Ecumenism," Religion News Service, February 25, 2021, https://religionnews.com/2021/02/25/the-insurrectionists-senate-floor-prayer-highlights-a-curious-trumpian-ecumenism.

3. Gina Ciliberto and Stephanie Russell-Kraft, "They Invaded the Capitol Saying 'Jesus Is My Savior. Trump Is My President,'" *Sojourners*, January 7, 2021, https://sojo.net/articles/they-invaded-capitol-saying-jesus-my-savior-trump-my-president.

4. *Encyclopaedia Britannica Online*, s.v. "Critical Race Theory," last updated October 25, 2023, https://www.britannica.com/topic/critical-race-theory.

Chapter 9 Know Peace, Know Justice

1. Martin Luther King Jr., "Letter from Birmingham Jail," August 1963, available at https://www.csuchico.edu/iege/_assets/documents/susi-letter-from-birmingham-jail.pdf.

2. Yana Jenay (@yanajenay), "Welcome to my brain. Every now and again, I hear something," Instagram, October 25, 2022, https://www.instagram.com/reel/CkJxPkoDYbm.

Chapter 10 "Go and Do Likewise"

1. St. Teresa of Ávila, quoted in Mark Etling, "Christ Has No Body on Earth But Yours," *National Catholic Reporter*, January 21, 2020, https://www.ncronline.org/spirituality/soul-seeing/soul-seeing/christ-has-no-body-earth-yours.

2. "ἔλεος," Blue Letter Bible, accessed February 8, 2024, https://www.blueletterbible.org/lexicon/g1656/kjv/tr/0-1.

Chapter 11 Beloved before Anything

1. Nelson Mandela, *Nelson Mandela by Himself: The Authorised Book of Quotations*, ed. Sello Hatang and Sahm Venter (Johannesburg, South Africa: Pan Macmillan South Africa, 2011), 116.

2. "σπλαγχνίζομαι," Blue Letter Bible, accessed February 8, 2024, https://www.blueletterbible.org/lexicon/g4697/kjv/tr/0-1.

3. These words come from the song "Thank You Jesus for the Blood," written by Charity Gayle, Ryan Kennedy, Steven Musso, David Gentiles, and Bryan McCleery, *Endless Praise* album, 2021.

Chapter 12 Being Sanctuaries

1. "Lord, Prepare Me to Be a Sanctuary" by Randy Scruggs and John Thompson, © 1982 Whole Armor Music and Full Armor Music.

2. *Merriam-Webster*, s.v. "sanctuary," accessed February 8, 2024, https://www.merriam-webster.com/dictionary/sanctuary.

3. Esther Lightcap Meek, *A Little Manual for Knowing* (Eugene, OR: Wipf & Stock, 2014), 74.

Pricelis Perreaux-Dominguez (MSW, MSEd) is a truthteller and space builder committed to helping the Body of Christ be healthy and holy. She is the founder of Full Collective, creator of the annual Sowers Summit, and host of the *Being a Sanctuary* podcast. She is currently pursuing a master of arts in biblical and theological studies from Denver Seminary and is a proud Black Latina (Dominicana) born and raised in New York City, where she resides with her husband and son.

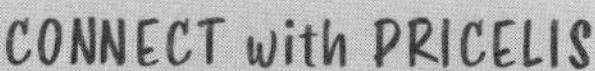

pricelispd.com